DISCIPLED WARRIORS

DISCIPLED WARRIORS

Growing Healthy Churches That Are Equipped for Spiritual Warfare

CHUCK LAWLESS

Discipled Warriors: Growing Healthy Churches That Are Equipped for Spiritual Warfare

Published by Kregel Publications, a division of Kregel, Inc., P.O. Box 2607, Grand Rapids, MI 49501. For more information about Kregel Publications, visit our Web site: www.kregel.com.

Cover design: John M. Lucas

Library of Congress Cataloging-in-Publication Data
Lawless, Charles E.
Discipled warriors: growing healthy churches that are equipped for spiritual warfare / by Chuck Lawless
p. cm.
Includes bibliographical references and indexes.
1. Spiritual Warfare. I. Title.
BV4509.5 .L39 2002 253–dc21
2002015469

ISBN 0-8254-3159-x

Printed in the United States of America

02 03 04 05 / 5 4 3 2 1

To Katherine Langford
and to the memory of Lawrence Langford,
who first introduced me to the book of Joshua
and the joy of victory in Christ,
and, as always,
to Pam, my wife

Contents

Table of Exhibits

FOREWORD

On rare occasions, I read a unique book by a unique author. Now, anyone who has ever been in a bookstore or other place that sells books knows that there is no scarcity of books. But there is no abundance of good books. In your hands is a good book—a very good book.

Chuck Lawless has done an incredible job of painting a picture of the healthy church. His thesis is that healthy churches produce true disciples who engage in and win the battles of spiritual warfare. Perhaps you have read works on spiritual warfare. You have encountered books on church health. And certainly there are many books on making disciples in the church. In *Discipled Warriors,* you have a work that rightly brings together all of these topics in a highly readable, intensely biblical, and demonstrably practical form.

I have a clear advantage in reading this book. I know Chuck Lawless. Indeed, I know Chuck Lawless well. I have seen how God continues to use him all over the world and how his impact on the world is growing each year. From several years ago when Chuck was my doctoral student until today when he is recognized as one of the leaders in addressing church health, church growth, and spiritual warfare, I have seen the hand of God upon him and his ministry.

May I offer a challenge to you, the reader? Before you begin reading *Discipled Warriors,* take time to pray. Ask God to open your heart to the information that you will read. Have a Bible alongside as you read. I can promise that your life will be changed. And I can promise that the material in this book can change your church as well.

On rare occasions, a book comes along that makes a big difference. You have in your hands such a book. Read it with a prayerful spirit. Read it for joy. But, above all, read it with the hope, knowledge, and promise that God will change your life through these pages.

—THOM S. RAINER, Dean

Billy Graham School of Missions, Evangelism and Church Growth

The Southern Baptist Theological Seminary, Louisville, Kentucky

Introduction

Have you ever faced a struggle when you tried to lead a church to growth? Has it ever seemed as though supernatural forces were doing everything possible to keep your church from growing? Jesus promised that the gates of Hades ultimately would not stand against His church (Matt. 16:18), but He never promised that we wouldn't face very real battles.

God's people will win, but not without first wrestling against the forces of darkness (Eph. 6:12). The Enemy wars against any church that seeks to grow for God's glory. Regrettably, he often wins battles simply because we are unprepared for the conflict.

This book is born out of my longing to see churches become healthy enough to win the battles of spiritual warfare *as they grow*. I hope that you're reading this book because you also long to see churches that glorify God and overcome the Enemy. Thanks for joining me in this challenge.

Church Growth in a New Millennium

I believe in church growth. As a member of the pastoral staff of a local church, I preach church growth. As a seminary professor, I promote the use of church growth principles, properly understood and rightly applied. Nevertheless, I fear that church growth principles sometimes are being abused to produce something other than a biblical church.

The strength of church growth principles is that they are effective in growing a church. The inherent danger of the principles, though, is that they might be used to grow a crowd rather than a church. Church members, if biblically and theologically ill-equipped, often don't recognize the difference between the two.

The current interest in "church health" has been, for the most part, a positive response to this problem.[1] More and more pastors are leading their churches to evaluate their purposes and programs biblically. A healthy church—one that balances worship, evangelism, discipleship, ministry, and fellowship—is assumed to be a growing church.

In this book, though, I raise three concerns about current "healthy church" models. First, I'm concerned that too little attention has been given to the theological foundation required for any healthy church. A weak foundation can support only a weak structure, and far too many churches that appear otherwise "healthy" lack a solid foundation.

Second, I contend that prayer is so evident in the early church that prayer itself should be a purpose of the church (e.g., Acts 2:42–47).[2] Particularly against the backdrop of church growth strategies and methods that often neglect spiritual realities, we need a renewed focus on prayer.

Third, I believe that including "discipleship" only as a segmented purpose of the church misses the biblical teaching that disciplemaking is much broader than a program or strategy.[3] Indeed, biblical discipling encompasses all purposes of the church, as we will see in chapter 2. While I am certain most writers addressing the purposes of the church recognize this fact, I'm afraid that discipleship remains more a program than a lifestyle. Consequently, we have had, in the words of Jim Peterson, "years of discipleship programs, and we are not discipled."[4]

Spiritual Warfare, Discipleship, and Church Growth

In 1955, Donald A. McGavran published *The Bridges of God*, the work on missions theory that gave birth to the Church Growth Movement.[5] McGavran, a mission administrator in India, sought to discover factors that helped or hindered growth in the stations for which he was responsible. Among other findings, he determined that the concept of *evangelism* had become so broad that the term carried little meaning. This central task had become secondary to other activities.[6] Missionaries were erecting hospitals, starting orphanages, and building schools, but they weren't reaching lost people and producing followers of Christ.

McGavran called for a return to legitimate evangelism; in fact, he coined the term *church growth* to refer to evangelism that results in fruit-bearing disciples of Christ. Church growth was to be measured not in "decisions" but in "disciples."

Two years before publication of *The Bridges of God*, Alan Redpath of the Moody Memorial Church in Chicago preached a series of sermons on the book of Joshua. Those sermons became the core of Redpath's 1955 book *Victorious Christian Living: Studies in the Book of Joshua*.[7] A Christian couple (to whom this book is dedicated) gave me a copy of Redpath's book when I was a teenager struggling with God's call. From that first reading, I developed an interest in the reality of spiritual battles and the call to victory in the Christian life.

Little did I realize then that the topic of spiritual warfare would gain a significant audience in the 1990s. In fact, more than one hundred books about warfare were published in that decade. Stimulated in part by the novels that Frank Peretti first published in the 1980s, several of these works had remarkable popular appeal.[8]

Some church growth leaders tend to see evangelism at the beginning of the new century in terms of spiritual warfare. Church growth leader C. Peter Wagner has argued that church growth principles are often ineffective unless they take into account the spiritual battlefield on which the secular person must be approached:

> I don't think there's anything wrong with the church growth principles we've developed, or the evangelistic techniques we're using. Yet somehow they don't seem to work. Maybe something else is needed so these principles we've been diligently working on will have better effect out in the marketplace. The real battle is now a spiritual battle, and as we are learning how to fight and win those battles, we are going to open the way for evangelistic techniques to have a much greater influence on our society than we've seen before.[9]

This battle is real. We wrestle "not against flesh and blood, but against the rulers, against the powers, against the world forces of this darkness, against the spiritual forces of wickedness in the heavenly places" (Eph. 6:12). We can't ignore the reality of spiritual warfare as we grow healthy, biblical churches.

At the same time, the biblical church must do spiritual warfare in a biblical manner. It is at this point that I part company with some leaders in the spiritual warfare movement. While many believers err in ignoring Satan, others err in giving him too much attention.[10] A decreased focus on God—albeit unintentional—often follows. Warfare strategies often focus more on our power, rather than on our weakness and God's strength (2 Cor. 12:9). Contemporary approaches to warfare assume at best, and ignore at worst, the necessity of spiritual disciplines as armor against Satan's wiles.

As I will contend in chapter 2, the process of "putting on the armor" (Eph. 6:10–17) is essentially biblical, lifestyle discipleship. Churches that miss this point fail to recognize the significance of discipleship in preparation for spiritual battles. They send believers into the battle unarmed. Should we be surprised, then, when our undiscipled members live defeated, discouraged lives?

Ministry in the Local Church

My concerns expressed in this book are driven by love for the local congregation. God privileged me to serve as a pastor for fourteen years in Ohio before I joined the faculty at Southern Seminary. Now I serve as a church staff member and a professor.

You will recognize that this book is both theological *and* practical. As noted, I believe that the church that lacks a solid theological foundation fails to function as the church should; in fact, a significant portion of chapter 1 is devoted to this issue. A solid foundation does not, however, eliminate our responsibility to build with appropriate and effective means upon that foundation.

The "how?" questions of church growth are important, and proper attention to methods and strategies does not automatically compromise theological integrity. Local churches must learn how to reach and disciple their communities while maintaining a biblical foundation. For this reason, this book includes suggestions for disciplemaking. Consider some strategies that you may have never before tried as you reflect on each chapter.

The Direction of This Book

Bringing together these three streams of church growth, spiritual warfare, and local church ministry is not a simple task. Still, I have attempted to do so in a helpful manner.

Chapter 1 lays the foundation for a biblical model for the local church. Chapter 2 presents discipleship as an overall goal, with emphasis on the armor of Ephesians 6. Defeating the Enemy through a discipled lifestyle—rather than through popular, power-driven approaches—is the focus.

Chapters 3 through 8 focus on the six purposes of the local congregation. Each chapter provides resources and strategies for growing a biblical church by producing spiritually armed disciples. For example, one purpose of the church is worship. We will answer several questions: What is worship? How is worship an element of disciple building? How does Satan strike against worship? What steps might the local church take to produce armed disciples who worship properly?

Chapters 9 and 10 deal with the process of becoming a disciplemaking church that threatens the Enemy. These chapters are my answer to the question "How do we move our church in the direction of this model?" Chapter 9 looks at leading through this change, and chapter 10 lays down a challenge for leaders.

You will better understand this book if you know some of the presuppositions and limitations that constrain and shape what is discussed. First, this book focuses on Satan's strategies, but I recognize that we battle primarily against the flesh and the world (Eph. 2:1–3). Our greatest enemy is the flesh (Rom. 7:14, 18; 8:1–17; Gal. 5:19–21). Satan often wins because we are easy prey, and the church is vulnerable because church members leave the gate open.

Second, although the Bible differentiates between *Satan* and *demons* (Matt. 12:22–29; 25:41), I use the terms interchangeably to describe forces of evil. Demons carry out the work of Satan.

Third, spiritual warfare is not about *reacting* to the Enemy—it is about putting on the armor of God in preparation for the battle. The church, rather than the Enemy, should have the upper hand in the battle by standing armed against the Devil's attacks.

Fourth, this discussion will not describe all of Satan's strategies nor all the ways in which we must counter him. The subject here is confined to Satan's attacks against the six purposes of the church. This is a narrow slice of Satan's overall initiative against the body of Christ. Sometimes his schemes overlap, for example striking at a church's worship in a way that damages fellowship.

Fifth, no reader will agree with every idea in the suggested resources. I certainly do not. However, in each source there is valuable information.

Acknowledgments

I could not have completed this work without the support of many people. To those churches who privileged me to be their pastor, I always will be grateful that you trusted me, loved me, challenged me, and believed in me.

My colleagues at Southern Seminary are the greatest. I thank you for your support. Tim Beougher and Tom Schreiner gave valuable suggestions for improving this work. I am especially grateful to Dean Thom Rainer for his suggestions and willingness to write the foreword. In addition, I thank my students for their continual support and their willingness to evaluate my ideas in the classroom.

An editor often makes invaluable contributions. Although I am responsible for weaknesses of this book, it is better because of the keen insights of my editor, Jim Weaver, and his staff. Thank you, Jim, for your guidance.

No words can express my gratitude and love for my wife, Pam. She has shared her time with this book—always supportive, even when she deserved more attention and time. Thank you, Pam, for loving me and for pushing me to fulfill God's call in my life.

And, finally, to you, the reader, thank you for investing your time. I pray that you and your church will be better armed for the battle when you have finished.

Notes

1. See, for example, Rick Warren, *The Purpose Driven Church* (Grand Rapids: Zondervan, 1995).

2. I am indebted to Thom Rainer, dean of the Billy Graham School of Missions, Evangelism and Church Growth of The Southern Baptist Theological Seminary, for this insight.
3. See Bill Hull, *The Disciplemaking Church* (Tarrytown, N.Y.: Revell, 1990).
4. Jim Peterson, *Lifestyle Discipleship* (Colorado Springs: NavPress, 1993), 15.
5. Donald A. McGavran, *The Bridges of God* (New York: Friendship Press, 1955).
6. Ibid., 53–54.
7. Alan Redpath, *Victorious Christian Living: Studies in the Book of Joshua* (Grand Rapids: Revell, 1955).
8. For example, Peretti's *This Present Darkness* (Westchester, Ill.: Crossway, 1986) and *Piercing the Darkness* (Westchester, Ill.: Crossway, 1989) had by mid-1996 sold a combined 3.7 million copies. Anderson's *The Bondage Breaker* had by mid-1997 sold 675,000 copies.
9. C. Peter Wagner, quoted in Ken Sidey, "Church Growth Finetunes Its Formulas," *Christianity Today*, 24 June 1991, 46–47.
10. C. S. Lewis, *The Screwtape Letters* (New York: Macmillan, 1961), 3.

CHAPTER 1

Establishing the Foundation of a Church

The discussion was strong, if not heated, at the pastors' conference. The guest speaker was uncompromising in his opinion: "A healthy church will be a growing church, and any church that isn't growing is somehow unhealthy." Several pastors agreed; others forcefully disagreed.

Jim, the pastor of a small country church in a dying town, was one who differed. His members were working hard to grow their church. They invited their friends and neighbors. Their fellowship was warm. Still, their best efforts couldn't stem the exodus from their town. Was Jim's church unhealthy, or was he just pastoring in unfertile territory?

Issues raised at that gathering are frequently debated. What is a "healthy" church? What are the purposes of the church? What constitutes a "growing" church? Is a healthy church always expanding numerically? Seldom is there complete agreement on the answers to any of these questions. For example, scholars and practitioners offer various analyses on what key elements comprise the purposes of the church. In *The Purpose Driven Church,* Rick Warren popularized the issue of church health through five purposes: (1) worship; (2) evangelism; (3) discipleship; (4) ministry; and (5) fellowship.[1] Theologian Wayne Grudem writes of three purposes: (1) ministry to God (worship); (2) ministry to believers (nurture); and (3) ministry to the world (evangelism and mercy).[2] Millard Erickson describes four purposes: (1) evangelism; (2) edification of believers (including discipleship and fellowship); (3) worship; and (4) social concern.[3]

Differences also surround the characteristics of what makes a church "healthy." Warren is among many who contend that a healthy church is one that balances attention among the purposes.[4] Others, such as Steven Macchia[5] and Christian Schwartz,[6] offer varied indicators (Exhibit 1-1).

Exhibit 1-1 Characteristics of a Healthy Church

Steven Macchia	Christian Schwartz
• God-empowering presence	• Empowering leadership
• God-exalting worship	• Gift-oriented ministry
• Attention to spiritual disciplines	• Passionate spirituality
• Learning and growing in community	• Functional structures
• Community of loving, caring relationships	• Inspiring worship services
• Servant-leadership development	• Holistic small groups
• Wise administration with accountability	• Needs-oriented
• Networking within the body	• Evangelism
• Stewardship and generosity	• Loving relationships

With all of these approaches to church health and church growth, why should there be another book to address the same issues? First, many current approaches to church health wrongly assume that each church adopting that approach desires to be a biblically sound, New Testament church. Little attention is given to the theological foundation of a church–which is, in my judgment, a critical error.

Second, while church growth theories that address the purposes of the church are important, further attention to these purposes is needed. Specifically, clarification and application of each of these purposes under the umbrella of New Testament "disciplemaking" is in order, as the next chapter will suggest.

Third, only a biblically healthy church will win the very real spiritual battles that we face daily; thus, biblical church health is a serious matter. The healthy church produces Christian disciples who are prepared for a spiritual war.

Outline of the Model

The model offered in this chapter (Exhibit 1-2) is an attempt to respond to each of the above concerns. This model is not the only pattern for the church, but I do believe it offers direction for the congregation that desires to be a healthy church winning spiritual warfare.

Four essential elements of the model are evident:

1. The *foundation* is just that–the bedrock on which the model itself stands. As we will see, the foundation must be biblically and theologically sound, focusing on our knowing God and our identity in Him. The first three chapters of the book of Ephesians provide the biblical support for this approach.
2. The *pillars* represent the purposes of the church as described in the Scriptures, particularly the Great Commission (Matt. 28:18–20), the Great Commandment (Matt. 22:35–40), and the portrayal of the early church (Acts 2:41–47). I'll explain these purposes more thoroughly throughout this book, but it may be helpful now to know the purposes proposed: *exalting* God through worship (Matt. 22:36–37, Acts 2:43, 47); *evangelizing* the world through proclamation and missions (Matt. 28:18–20, Acts 2:41, 47); *equipping* believers through teaching and mentoring (Matt.

28:18–20, Acts 2:42); *edifying* one another through ministry and service (Matt. 22:39, Acts 2:44–45); *encountering* God through prayer (Acts 2:42); and *encouraging* one another through fellowship (Acts 2:42, 46).

3. The *roof* represents the external component of this model; that is, this section answers the question, "Where should the truths of this model become evident in my individual life?" The last three chapters of Ephesians (4–6) provide a biblical answer to this question. Specifically, these chapters demand a faith that affects all of our life. Our personal walk with God is to be evident in our family, our church, and our workplace.
4. The *cross* at the top of the model reminds us that our mandate as a biblical church is to proclaim the gospel to the world. A healthy church always looks beyond itself to fulfill the Great Commission.

The Foundation: Biblical Truth Lived Out

ChurchWorks: A Well-Body Book for Congregations is designed to help leaders "take charge of the health and well-being of your congregation."[7] At first glance, the book gives generally good suggestions for growing a congregation, including:

- Have written policies for personnel, committees, by-laws, and other matters.
- Have balance and symmetry in corporate worship, limiting such distractions as announcements.
- Organize affinity groups for fellowship.
- Have a vision and carry out mission beyond your congregation.
- Use lay ministers to carry out ministry.

But a problem becomes apparent when one realizes that the author writes out of presuppositions as a Unitarian Universalist

Exhibit 1-2 The Church Model

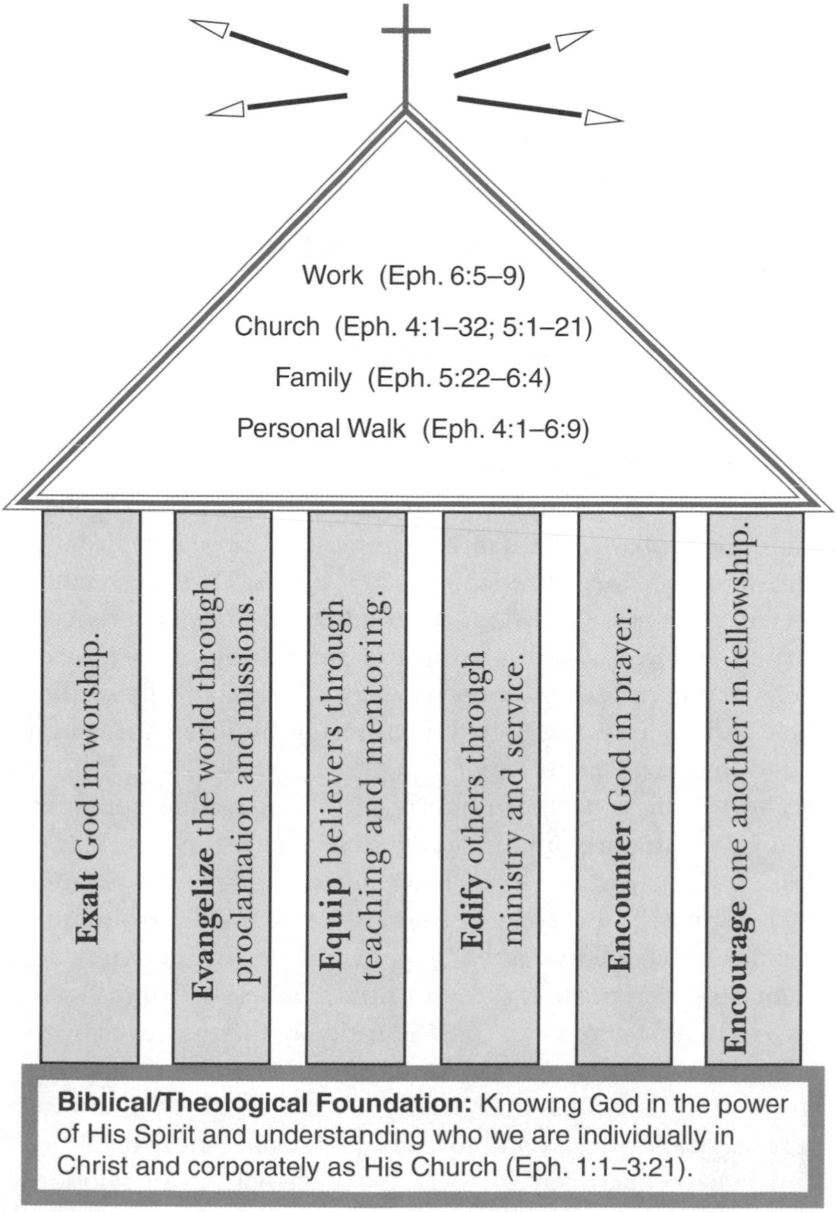

Work (Eph. 6:5–9)

Church (Eph. 4:1–32; 5:1–21)

Family (Eph. 5:22–6:4)

Personal Walk (Eph. 4:1–6:9)

Exalt God in worship.

Evangelize the world through proclamation and missions.

Equip believers through teaching and mentoring.

Edify others through ministry and service.

Encounter God in prayer.

Encourage one another in fellowship.

Biblical/Theological Foundation: Knowing God in the power of His Spirit and understanding who we are individually in Christ and corporately as His Church (Eph. 1:1–3:21).

who is promoting religious pluralism and inclusive humanism. Freedom of lifestyle is assumed without regard to biblical truth, and "spirituality" is generic. Thus, this work fails to promote the most basic component of congregational health—a biblical understanding of Christianity and the church. The reality is that following the principles in *ChurchWorks* may help a congregation to grow, but the result will not be a New Testament church.

The Importance of a Biblical Foundation

Sadly, not all believers in evangelical churches are biblically literate enough to recognize the theological problems with such a book. Because so few churches offer solid biblical and theological training, we have produced generations of believers who have a weak foundation for their faith.

Recently, I asked about twenty members of an evangelical church how many of them had completed a course in basic Christian doctrine. Three raised their hands. Had these members all been new Christians, I wouldn't have been overly concerned. However, some of them were long-term church members, even leaders, who had never systematically studied their basic beliefs. Their story, I suspect, is duplicated throughout evangelical Christianity.

The weakness of the modern church is readily apparent. Church attendance among adults declined in the first half of the 1990s and did not experience significant growth through the latter half of the decade.[8] In many cases, membership numbers far exceed actual attendance. Lifestyles of members are often no different than those of nonmembers. George Barna reports that 34 percent of those identifying themselves as born-again believers believe that they will go to heaven because they are basically good people.[9] George Gallup adds that, among persons who express some sort of religious preference, 63 percent believe that both Christian and non-Christian religions offer true paths to God. Only 41 percent of those identifying themselves as born-again Christians believe Satan is a real being, and only 36 percent of mainline attenders believe strongly that the Bible is totally accurate.[10]

At the risk of oversimplifying the issues leading to this situation, *we simply haven't built a strong biblical foundation.* Churches without a biblical foundation have little to offer to a world searching for purpose. They certainly don't alarm Satan very much.

Jesus Christ is both the cornerstone and the head of the church (Eph. 2:20; 5:23), but it is through the Scriptures that we know Him. Divinely—and thus perfectly—inspired (2 Tim. 3:16–17), the Word of God "as the expression of God's will to us, possesses the right supremely to define what we are to believe and how we are to conduct ourselves."[11]

For that reason, we will begin with the foundation of a church rather than its purposes. Only the church that accepts and follows God's Word as authoritative will ever be healthy.

Background from Ephesians

The basic outline of the book of Ephesians provides the foundation and roof for the church model. Written to a society not unlike contemporary North America, Ephesians offers hope and direction for a church facing daily spiritual battles. The believers around Ephesus lived in a pagan, if "spiritual," society.[12] Magical occultism was common. Belief in both good and evil powers influenced every area of life. Worship of the goddess Diana dominated the area, and more than forty other gods were worshiped in the city.[13] New believers coming from this power-oriented society faced intense spiritual battles.

Paul's letter, however, in essence assured the believers, "You are in Christ (Eph. 1:1), and He has already conquered the powers (vv. 18–23). The battle is still real, but victory is assured." Meanwhile, the believers were to put on their armor and stand firm against the Enemy (6:11).

The theological base

To appreciate how much help we can draw from Ephesians, we need to understand the general outline of Paul's letter. In the first three chapters, Paul laid the theological foundation for victory in spiritual warfare: *Believers are in Christ.* We are chosen *in Him* (Eph. 1:4) and have redemption through *His* blood (v. 7). *In Him* we have an inheritance (v. 10–11). We have our hope *in Him* and have been sealed *in Him* (vv. 12–13). We are created *in Him* for good works (2:10). *In Him* we have been given life (1:20; 2:5–7). *Through Him* we have access to God (v. 18).

This *theological* truth—that believers find security in their identity in Christ—is foundational for the book of Ephesians (see Exhibit 1–3). Standing on this theological truth enabled the Ephesians to stand firm against the schemes of Satan. Likewise, the healthy church must first have a theological foundation based upon knowing God and who they are individually and corporately in Christ. It is He who gives us power to win the battles (Eph. 1:18–19; 3:14–21).

Exhibit 1-3 The Foundation of the Church Model

Biblical/Theological Foundation: Knowing God in the power of His Spirit and understanding who we are individually in Christ and corporately as His Church (Eph. 1:1–3:21).

The practical application

The final three chapters of Ephesians build upon the theological foundation of Ephesians 1–3. The emphasis shifts from the theological to the practical, and these chapters flesh out the believer's victory in Christ.

Paul described a life characterized by church unity (Eph. 4:1–16; see also 2:11–18), personal holiness (4:17–5:20), and Christ-like relationships in the home (5:22–6:4) and in the workplace (6:5–9). Our position in Christ produces a life characterized by righteousness, truth, wholesome speaking, kindness, thanksgiving, a forgiving spirit, and loving submission to each other in godliness (4:1–6:9). Old patterns of callousness, sensuality, greed, deceit, anger, theft, bitterness, immorality, coarse jesting, and drunkenness must be forsaken (4:17–5:20).

Paul essentially said to the Ephesians, "Who you are in Christ must affect every area of your life." That admonition is the basis for the roof on this model. Built upon a solid biblical and theological foundation, our faith must affect our personal walk (Eph. 4:1–6:9) at home (5:22–6:4), church (4:1–5:21), and workplace (6:5–9). Believers must walk "in a manner worthy of the calling with which you have been called" (4:1; see Exhibit 1-4).

Leaders then must ask, "Do we as a body help members to

Exhibit 1-4 The Rooftop of the Church Model

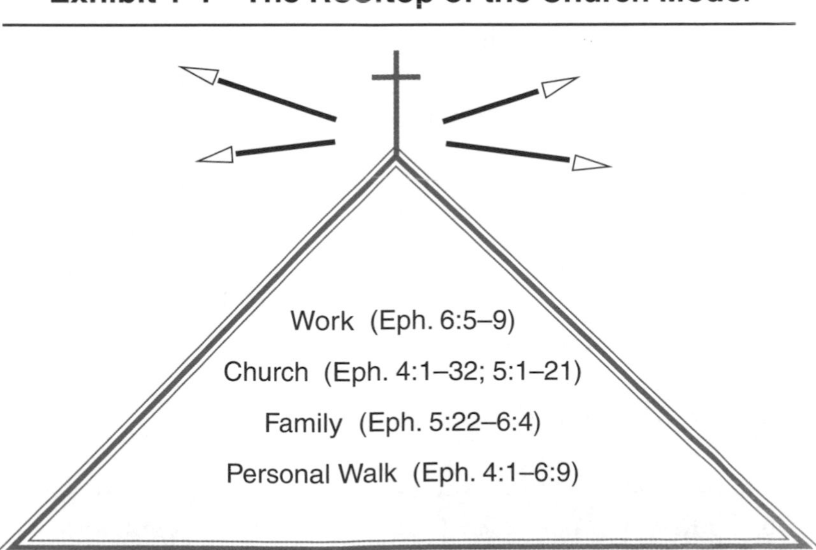

live out their faith in *all* areas of life?" To assume that church members automatically apply our teachings in every area is naïve. Just as Paul applied his teaching specifically to the Ephesians' lives, we should guide people to do the same.

Take, for example, the "work" component of this model. A healthy church trains members to influence their workplace. This training might take the form of a class on how to start a workplace Bible study or scheduling a time when members would come together to pray for the people with whom they work. Members living out their faith at work are obedient to the demands of Ephesians 6:5–9. The continual challenge for a church is to develop a comprehensive strategy that addresses *all* of the areas noted in Ephesians while maintaining a solid biblical and theological foundation.

The spiritual battle

Leading a church to build a theological foundation, to apply biblical truth in all of life, and to fulfill all of its purposes is not easy. Satan is "seeking someone to devour" (1 Peter 5:8). He wants believers to question God's Word and make choices independent of it (see Gen. 3:1–7). He doesn't want the church to be healthy, so he wars against all attempts to fulfill its mission (see Exhibit 1-5).

What do we do about the Enemy's strategies? Putting on the "full armor of God" in preparation for spiritual battles (Eph. 6:11) was imperative for the Ephesians. It remains imperative for us. The healthy church produces discipled warriors who stand against the schemes of the Enemy.

Applying the Foundation

We have observed that the healthy church must first have a solid biblical and theological foundation that focuses on knowing God and who we are in Christ. Those foundational truths are

Exhibit 1-5 Enemy Arrows Against the Church

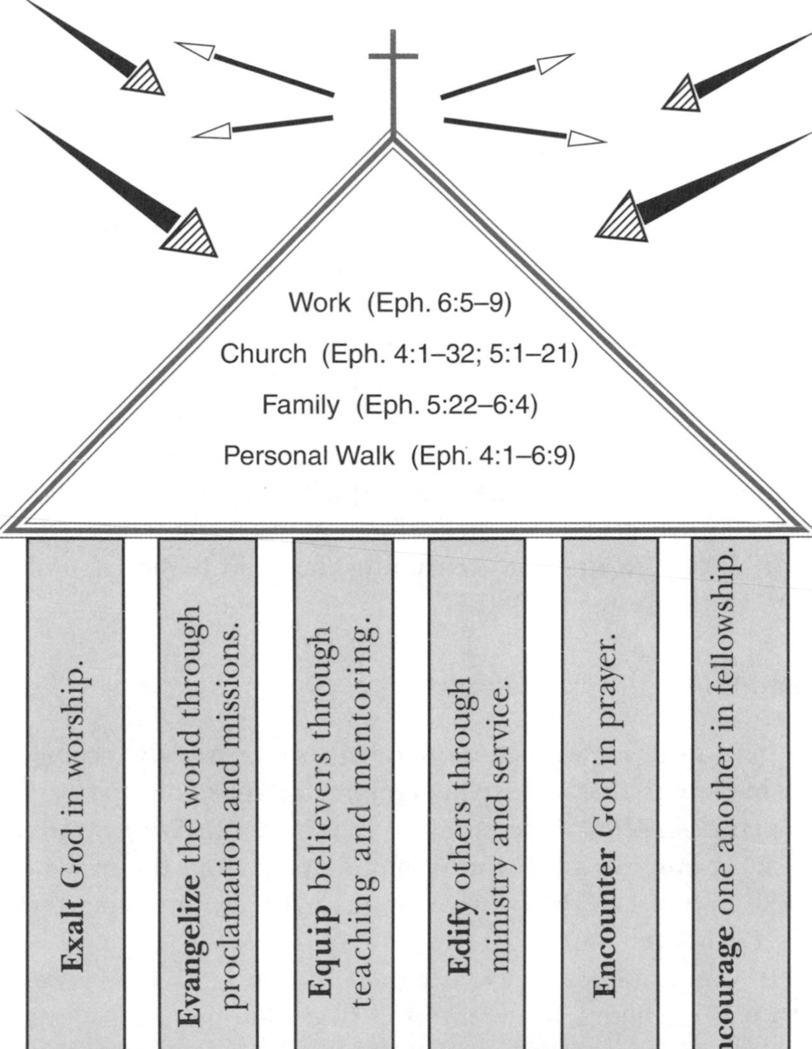

Biblical/Theological Foundation: Knowing God in the power of His Spirit and understanding who we are individually in Christ and corporately as His Church (Eph. 1:1–3:21).

what we live out, enabled as a healthy church fulfills its purposes. Think again about what that position means, according to Ephesians 1–3.

Our focus must be on God alone.

The book of Ephesians gave hope to believers who faced daily battles against spiritual powers, but the letter is not about the powers. The principalities and powers pale in the presence of the King who reigns (Eph. 1:21). *His* power enables growth and fruitfulness in our lives (3:16, 20–21). The armor we are to wear is *His* armor, not ours (6:13).

Obviously Ephesians (and the rest of the Bible) is about God, but we often make plans without seeking God's direction. We preach more about human needs than about the grace of God. Churches that are enthused about spiritual warfare focus more on Satan's strategies than on God's solutions. A counterdirection is in order, starting with reframing the solid biblical foundation and focusing on God.

Salvation is in Christ alone.

In a world where religious pluralism is increasingly accepted, it's imperative that we keep in mind that our position "in Christ" depends on Him alone (John 14:6; Acts 4:12). We who were dead in our sins were without hope apart from the grace of God (Eph. 2:1–9). Only by grace through faith in Him are we "in Christ" (vv. 8–9).

In Christ, we are graciously the children of God. We were "by nature children of wrath," but God loved us with a "great love" (Eph. 2:3–4) that "surpasses knowledge" (3:19). God chose and adopted us "according to the kind intention of His will" (1:4–5). He gave us eternal life and made us "fellow citizens with the saints" (2:19). His love is so great for us that we ultimately cannot comprehend its magnitude.

Furthermore, we are sealed in Him with the Spirit (Eph. 1:13). We have been created in Him for good works (2:10). He alone is the cornerstone (v. 20); it is He who puts the church together (vv. 20–22). A healthy church teaches that eternal salvation is available only through a personal relationship with Jesus.

Focusing on such grace has at least three benefits. First, believers who begin to understand the depth of God's grace are less likely to boast (Eph. 2:9). Pride weakens a church's health, producing strife and division (see 1 Cor. 1:11–13; 3:1–4; 11:18–19). Members who realize their worth only in God's grace serve with a Christlike humility. Second, believers who appreciate grace resist temptation. If I view my sin as offending a holy God who died for me (Rom. 5:8), I should be willing to sin less, not more (6:1–2).

Third, knowing who we are in Christ's grace helps us ward off other attacks.[14] Satan most often attacks with discouragement and defeat. Counter his attacks by standing on wondrous promises like these:

- We are God's children (Eph. 1:5).
- We have been bought with a price (1 Cor. 6:19–20).
- We have redemption and the forgiveness of sins (Col. 1:14).
- We have been sealed with His Spirit (2 Cor. 1:21–22).
- We can do all things through Him (Phil. 4:13).

In Christ, we have privileges and responsibilities.

No single description can fully capture the mystery of God's church, but some metaphors help us glimpse its reality.[15] In the book of Ephesians, the church is described as the body of Christ (1:22–23; 4:15–16), God's household (2:19), a building or holy temple (v. 21), and the bride of Christ (5:22–33).

The marriage imagery particularly shows us that we have privilege and responsibilities. As Christ's bride, we are privileged to be His beloved, whom He chose (Eph. 1:5). He gave

Himself for us to make us holy (5:25–27). He loves us with a sacrificial, all-consuming love. Someday, He will invite us to enjoy His full fellowship (Rev. 19:7–10).

Responsibility also is implied. The church is to be pure, fully devoted to Christ (see 2 Cor. 11:2). Faithfulness is assumed; spiritual adultery is not an option. Christ is the head of the church, and we are to submit willingly and unreservedly to His leadership (Eph. 5:23–24).

God grants us the privilege of being His bride while expecting the response of faithful, submissive love. This pattern of privilege and responsibility is evident in many New Testament pictures, as shown in Exhibit 1-6. Christians must recognize their privileges *and* fulfill their responsibilities.

Implications of these images are several. For example, a healthy church with a solid foundation must hold its members accountable. God demands holiness (Lev. 19:1–2). He expects His people to serve in their assigned places, or the entire body is damaged (1 Cor. 12:12–31a). The church that expects anything less from its members is not biblically healthy.

Many churches today are raising their expectations. In *High Expectations: The Remarkable Secret for Keeping People in Your Church*, Thom Rainer reports on assimilation rates of new members in 287 evangelistically growing churches. He concludes that churches assimilate new members more effectively when they expect more from their members.[16]

This move toward higher expectations, says Rainer, is increasingly evident: "Perhaps one of the most significant trends in the twenty-first century will be the clear expectations of church members to live for Christ in the context of their local churches."[17] Such a trend toward biblical church health is welcome.

Another implication of the New Testament description of the church is the need for training. A new Christian must be taught kingdom privileges and responsibilities. A young believer who desires to be holy might not know the Bible's teachings about particular sin issues. The believer needs guidance to know

Exhibit 1-6 The Church Is . . . Key New Testament Images

Metaphor	In Christ, we are . . .	Our Privileges	Our Responsibilities
Christ's Body Rom. 12:3–8; 1 Cor. 12:12–31; Eph. 1:22–23; 4:15–16; Col. 1:17–18	• members of His body. • uniquely gifted.	• to use our gifts in Christ's work • to be members of Christ's body	• to follow Christ as Head • to use gifts within the body • to be accountable to others • to be in fellowship with others
God's People 2 Cor. 6:16–18; Titus 2:14; Heb. 8:8–10; 1 Peter 2:9–10	• His people.	• to be chosen • to receive His attention and care • to be the "apple of his eye" (Deut. 32:10 KJV)	• to recognize His ownership • to obey Him • to be holy because He is holy (Lev. 19:2)
Temple of the Holy Spirit 1 Cor. 3:16–17; 6:19–20; Eph. 2:21–22	• vessels of the Holy Spirit.	• to be filled with His presence • to be given His power (Acts 1:8)	• to obey the Spirit (John 16:8–11) • to bear fruit (Gal. 5:22–23)
Royal Priesthood 1 Peter 2:9–12	• chosen to be God's priests in the world.	• to represent God among humanity • to proclaim His name	• to abstain from sin • to live as "aliens and strangers" (1 Peter 2:11)
Flock of His Pasture John 10:11–16; Acts 20:28; 1 Peter 5:1–4; Rev. 7:9–17	• Sheep—dependent on the Shepherd and humbly following.	• to be cared for and secure • to be led • to know the Shepherd's voice	• to submit to the Shepherd's voice • to trust His wisdom and guidance

where and how to serve. The church that holds members accountable to New Testament standards must equip them to meet those standards.

I was reminded of this critical issue as I taught the need to do evangelism in a new member class. I passionately exhorted members to share their faith. In the middle of my plea, a woman raised her hand. "I'm new at this whole thing," she began. "I don't even know what *evangelism* means, much less how to do it. What exactly is evangelism?"

I apologized to this woman. I had assumed knowledge that many do not have when they are new believers.

Finally, New Testament descriptions of the church show that God is the Head. We are *His* bride, *His* body, *His* priests, *His* temple, *His* sheep, and *His* people. All-powerful (Matt. 19:26) and all knowing (1 John 3:20), God owns His church. We who are His must not take our responsibilities lightly. Discipled warriors can stand when their foundation for life is the Word of God.

Application

Several years ago, I was living in a home in the Midwest, an area frequented by tornadoes. The home was built above a crawlspace. Neighbors and family members encouraged me to retreat to the crawlspace for safety when tornado warnings sounded.

Their suggestion made sense, except that the wooden flooring above the crawlspace had been weakened by water damage. Some of the main support beams were warped. Others had been partially destroyed by hungry termites. Portions of the plywood floor were almost gone. The flooring that essentially served as a foundation for the structure could not be trusted to provide protection when the storms came. To retreat there when the tornado sirens blared would have made little sense. No security exists when you can't trust the foundation on which you depend.

In contrast, Christians have a solid foundation on which we can build our lives and our churches. Healthy churches lead their members to know God in the power of His Spirit and to know who they are in Christ. Churches built upon scriptural truth produce believers who aren't afraid in the storm.

A church can strengthen its biblical and theological foundation in a number of ways. The following are a sample.

- Conduct a theological survey to identify deficiencies or errors among the people. Use the survey to determine specific issues to address. A few of the possible questions are suggested in Exhibit 1-7 (p. 38).
- Preach a series of sermons on the attributes of God.
- Teach through your tradition's creeds and catechisms or the congregation's own doctrinal statement.
- Lead a series of Bible studies on the images of the church in the New Testament.
- Develop a new member's class that strengthens the emphasis on doctrinal basics.
- Conduct a study on the "people of God" imagery in the Old Testament.
- Develop a series of lessons on the privileges of being *in Christ.*
- Determine the percentage of active attenders who are intentionally involved in ministry. Use this information to encourage all members to find their place in the body of Christ.
- Preach a sermon series on the authority of the Bible.
- Teach from Ephesians. Consider teaching points raised by this study.
- Develop a systematic approach for teaching the Bible to all ages.
- Evaluate membership standards and whether to "raise the bar."

Exhibit 1-7 Sample Questions for Member Survey

Circle the number that best characterizes your current beliefs regarding the following statements.

Jesus Christ is the Son of God.

strongly disagree	disagree	uncertain	agree with reservations	strongly agree
1	2	3	4	5

Good people who never hear of Jesus probably will go to heaven.

strongly disagree	disagree	uncertain	agree with reservations	strongly agree
1	2	3	4	5

Every member of a local church should do some service or ministry through the church.

strongly disagree	disagree	uncertain	agree with reservations	strongly agree
1	2	3	4	5

God and Satan are equally powerful.

strongly disagree	disagree	uncertain	agree with reservations	strongly agree
1	2	3	4	5

For further study

Anderson, Neil. *Victory over the Darkness: Realizing the Power of Your Identity in Christ*. Ventura, Calif.: Regal, 1990.

Basden, Paul A., and David S. Dockery, eds. *The People of God: Essays on the Believer's Church*. Nashville: Broadman & Holman, 1991.

Driver, John. *Images of the Church in Mission*. Scottdale, Pa: Herald, 1997.

Enns, Paul. *The Moody Handbook of Theology*. Chicago: Moody, 1989.

Getz, Gene, and Joseph Wall. *Effective Church Growth Strategies*. Dallas: Word, 2000.

Hunter, Kent. *Foundations for Church Growth: Biblical Basics for the Local Church*. Corunna, Ind.: Church Growth Center, 1994.

Kaiser, Walter C. Jr. *Mission in the Old Testament: Israel as a Light to the Nations*. Grand Rapids: Baker, 2000.

Moreau, A. Scott. *Essentials of Spiritual Warfare*. Wheaton, Ill.: Harold Shaw, 1997.

Nash, Ronald A. *Is Jesus the Only Savior?* Grand Rapids: Zondervan, 1995.

Packer, J. I. *Knowing God*. Downers Grove, Ill.: InterVarsity, 1973.

Piper, John. *Desiring God*. Sisters, Ore: Multnomah, 1996.

Rainer, Thom S. *Effective Evangelistic Churches*. Nashville: Broadman & Holman, 1996.

——. *The Book of Church Growth*. Nashville: Broadman & Holman, 1993.

Robinson, Darrell. *Total Church Life: How to Be a First-Century Church*. Nashville: Broadman & Holman, 1997.

Notes

1. Rick Warren, *The Purpose Driven Church* (Grand Rapids: Zondervan, 1995), 103–6.
2. Wayne Grudem, *Systematic Theology* (Grand Rapids: Zondervan, 1994), 867–68.
3. Millard Erickson, *Christian Theology*, 2d ed. (Grand Rapids: Baker, 1998), 1061–69.
4. Warren, *Purpose Driven Church*, 17: "Church growth is the natural result of church health. Church health can occur only when our message is *biblical* and our mission is *balanced*. Each of the five New Testament purposes of the church must be in equilibrium with the others for the health to occur. Balance in the church does not occur naturally; in fact, we must continually correct imbalance. It is human nature to overemphasize the aspect of the church we feel most passionately about. Intentionally setting

up a strategy and a structure to force ourselves to give equal attention to each purpose is what being a purpose-driven church is all about."

Grudem, *Systematic Theology*, 868: "We should beware of any attempts to reduce the purpose of the church to only one of these three and to say that it should be our primary focus. In fact, such attempts to make one of these purposes primary will always result in some neglect of the other two. . . . All three purposes must be emphasized continually in a healthy church."

Erickson, *Christian Theology*, 1060: "The church has been charged to carry out Christ's ministry in the world. To accomplish this, certain functions must be met. A balance of these functions is essential to the spiritual health and well-being of the body."

5. Steven Macchia, *Becoming a Healthy Church* (Grand Rapids: Baker, 1999). Macchia's conclusions are based on the study of 100 churches visited in New England.
6. Christian Schwartz, *Natural Church Development* (Carol Stream, Ill.: ChurchSmart, 1998). Schwartz's research is based on the study of more than 1000 churches throughout the world. Though Schwartz's conclusions are not dissimilar to the findings of other studies, some writers have seriously questioned his research method. See, e.g., John Ellas and Flavil Yeakley, "A Book Review of *Natural Church Development*," *Journal of the American Society of Church Growth* (Spring 1999): 83–92. I include Schwartz's research simply because his findings are generally reflective of others writing in this field.
7. Anne Odin Heller, *Churchworks: A Well-Body Book for Congregations* (Boston: Skinner House, 1999), 9.
8. George Barna, "The State of the Church, 2000," Barna Research Online.
9. Barna, "Beliefs: Theological," Barna Research Online Archive Report.
10. George Gallup, "Religion," @ www.gallup.com/poll/indicators/indreligion.

11. Erikson, *Christian Theology*, 267.
12. Many scholars believe that Ephesians was an encyclical letter written to a number of churches.
13. Clinton E. Arnold, *Powers of Darkness: Principalities and Powers in Paul's Letters* (Downers Grove, Ill.: InterVarsity, 1992), 150.
14. This truth is the basis for many of the writings of Neil Anderson, who has written extensively about spiritual warfare. See *The Bondage Breaker* (Eugene, Ore.: Harvest House, 1993).
15. Paul S. Minear, *Images of the Church in the New Testament* (Philadelphia: Westminster, 1960).
16. Thom S. Rainer, *High Expectations: The Remarkable Secret for Keeping People in Your Church* (Nashville: Broadman & Holman, 1999), 22–23.
17. Ibid., 63.

CHAPTER 2

THE GOAL: DISCIPLED WARRIORS

Tim wasn't raised in a Christian home. He became a Christian at age twenty after a friend told him the good news of Christ's saving grace. Tim was baptized, joined the church, and within a few years was teaching a class for children.

But Tim was struggling in his own Christian walk. His devotions were sporadic. His prayer life was almost nonexistent. Witnessing was difficult, if not impossible. Failure to stand against temptations was habitual.

The problem, though, was not so much that Tim didn't want to be faithful. He did not *know how* to grow in Christ. Church leaders told him to read his Bible, but they gave him no guidance for doing so. They said, "Pray every day," but they didn't teach him to pray. Nobody trained him to share the gospel. When he faced temptation, no brother held him accountable. Tim's church had failed him.

Your church must avoid such mistakes. The healthy body produces *disciples* of Jesus rather than just converts. Only disciples can overcome the inevitable spiritual battles that all of us face.

The Great Commission–A Command to Do What?

Tim belonged to a body that might boast of being a "Great Commission" church. If so, they do not understand the thrust of Christ's instruction. Expressions of the Great Commission occur five times (Matt. 28:18–20; Mark 16:15; Luke 24:46–49; John 20:21; Acts 1:8).[1] The statements reveal five basic truths about the commission:

1. Christ is the authority who demands our obedience (Matt. 28:18; John 20:21).
2. Christ commissions us, and He is the focus of our message (Mark 16:15; Luke 24:46–47).
3. Preaching, teaching, and baptizing are strategies to fulfill the commission (Matt. 28:19–20; Mark 16:15; Luke 24:47).
4. The message we proclaim is for the world (Matt. 28:19–20; Mark 16:15; Luke 24:27; Acts 1:8).
5. Christ promises His power and presence as we go (Matt. 28:20; Luke 24:49; Acts 1:8).

All five statements of the Great Commission challenge us to be His witnesses to the world. Matthew's account, though, perhaps best describes our goal in fulfilling the commission. Around the world we are to make disciples who follow Christ's teachings.

> And Jesus came up and spoke to them saying, "All authority has been given to Me in heaven and on earth. Go therefore and make disciples of all the nations, baptizing them in the name of the Father and the Son and the Holy Spirit, teaching them to observe all that I commanded you; and lo, I am with you always, even to the end of the age." (Matt. 28:18–20)

The Nature of Discipleship

The term translated "disciple" throughout the New Testament is routinely used to describe a follower of Jesus in the Gospels and Acts.[2] The word is a derivative of a verb meaning "to learn." At the core of discipleship is learning from a teacher. A disciple was–and is–first a student.

Yet, biblical discipleship is much broader than intellectual learning. Biblical discipleship is a *lifestyle* best described in Jesus' words: "A pupil is not above his teacher; but everyone, after he has been fully trained, *will be like his teacher*" (Luke 6:40, emphasis added; see Matt. 9:9; 19:21; Mark 1:17, 2:14, 8:34; Luke 5:27; John 1:43). A disciple is a committed follower who seeks to model his life after his teacher.

The book of Acts considers followers of Jesus to be disciples (see, e.g., Acts 6:1; 9:1–2; 9:36; 11:26; 13:52; 14:20; 16:1). The book reveals a community of disciples whose *entire lives* were controlled by their commitment to Christ. They grew in faith as the church grew numerically. The early disciples were daily and continually being conformed to the image of Christ (Rom. 8:29). They were becoming discipled warriors.

The Process of Disciplemaking

Just as the command to "make disciples" is clearly stated by Matthew, the process of discipling is captured in the instructions "baptizing them" and "teaching them" in Matthew 28:19–20. Both components were, for the early church and still for us, necessary elements of discipleship.

Baptizing represented conversion and commitment to a crucified and resurrected Christ (Rom. 6:3–4). Obviously implied in this mandate is the task of evangelism. Believers in the early church announced the good news of Christ, nonbelievers repented and believed, and the new converts were then baptized (see Acts 2:37–38).

Teaching was the task of instructing. Teaching was not limited to imparting information; assumed in the teaching was a command *to obey* all that Jesus taught. Head knowledge was to become heart knowledge and changed lifestyle. In fact, obedience to the commands of Christ indicated the disciples' love for Him (John 14:15, 15:10).

Those who obey the Great Commission make disciples through evangelism, leading to baptism and teaching that result in obedience. Donald McGavran reminds us that legitimate church growth is Great Commission growth:

> Only where Christians constrained by love obediently press on, telling men the good news of the Savior, does the Church spread and increase. Where there is no faithfulness in proclaiming Christ, there is no growth. . . . Church growth follows where the lost are not merely found but restored to normal life in the fold—though it may be a life they have never consciously known. . . . When existing Christians, marching obediently under the Lord's command and filled with His compassion, fold the wanderers and feed the flock, then churches multiply; but when they indolently permit men and women who have made costly decisions for Christ to drift back into the world, then indeed churches do not grow.[3]

Challenges to Disciplemaking

Disciplemaking, as defined in Matthew 28, must be broader than a single purpose of the church if it includes both baptizing and teaching. If evangelism is a component of disciplemaking, it would seem illogical to include both evangelism and discipleship as purposes of the church, as many current models do. The breadth of "teaching them to observe all that I commanded you" (Matt. 28:20) suggests something much larger than a singular purpose among several equal purposes of the church. I will argue in chapter 5 that *equipping* is a better term for discipleship.

Making disciples is also an equipping *process* rather than a program. Baptism is an initiation rite of discipleship, but the process of teaching and obeying is continual. A disciple is always in the process of becoming like Jesus. In some churches, though, disciplemaking is a narrow training program with little focus or intention. Believers study randomly chosen, short-term courses, and those who complete the courses are "discipled." I affirm the validity of these short-term studies, but only within the context of an overall discipleship strategy addressing the totality of Christian living. I am particularly concerned that many of these discipleship programs don't include evangelism training. I've consulted with churches that train members in prayer, parenting, finances, and relationships, but they omit evangelism. Disciplemaking thus becomes inward focused, often missing entirely the "baptizing" element of the Great Commission.

Further, biblical disciplemaking assumes accountability. As we saw in the previous chapter, the biblical images of the church imply both privileges and responsibilities. One of those responsibilities is obedience to God, including obedience to the command to make disciples through baptizing and teaching.

The early church took seriously Jesus' mandate to obey His teachings and to teach others to obey. Conversion followed by baptism was followed by teaching that demanded obedience. Where obedience was not evident, the church took steps of discipline (e.g., 1 Cor. 5:1–5; 2 Thess. 3:14–15; 1 Tim. 1:18–20). The healthy church will likewise hold its members accountable to biblical standards.

A Model for Disciplemaking

The healthy church builds on its solid biblical and theological foundation to make disciples. Disciple-making bodies teach their members all that Jesus commanded. They teach the purposes of the church. They guide in learning to worship. They teach how to serve, evangelize, pray, equip, and fellowship. They help believers apply and evaluate this faith in every area of their lives.

This entire process—taking believers from theological foundation to practical living—is biblical disciplemaking, as indicated graphically by the lines added in Exhibit 2-1. This process of discipleship is never-ending and life-changing.

Exhibit 2-1 A Model for Disciplemaking

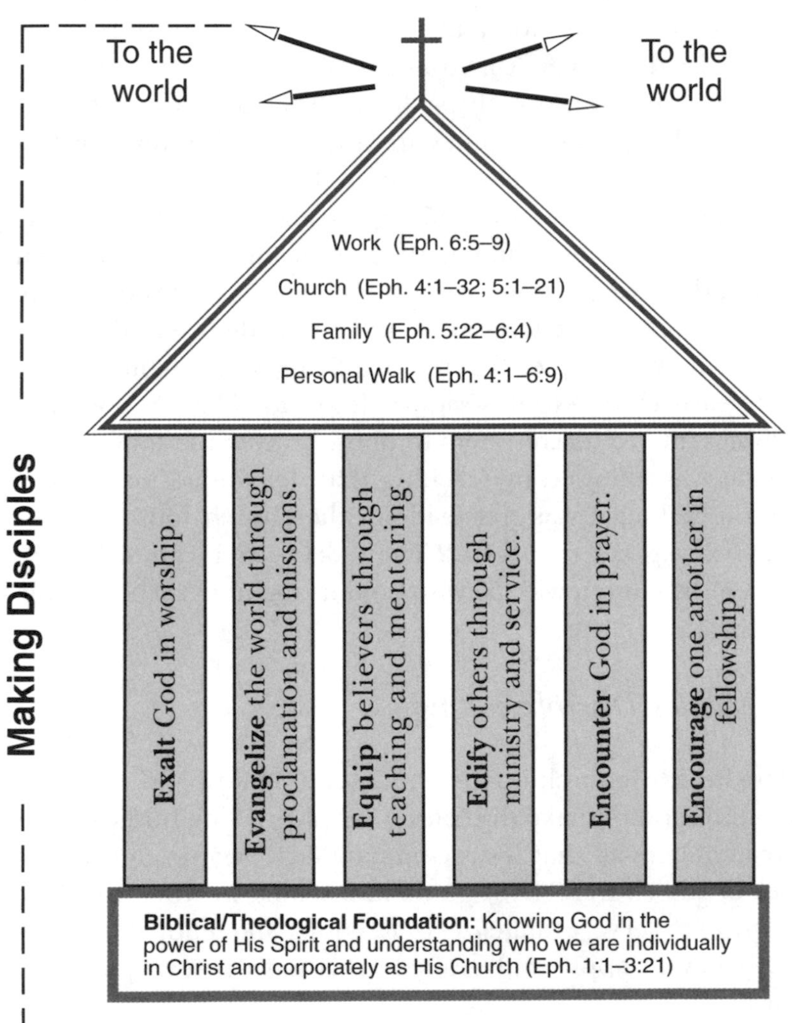

The Great Commission and Spiritual Warfare

With this model, a church evaluating its discipling strategy should ask:

- Are we teaching our members theologically? Are we challenging them to know God and who they are in Christ? Is their foundation solid?
- Do our members know the purposes of the church? Are we training them to fulfill those purposes individually and corporately?
- Do our members show their Christian faith in all areas of their lives—in their personal walk, in their home, in the church, and in their workplace? Are we teaching them to live out their faith in all of these areas?
- Are our members committed to reaching the world for Christ?
- In general, are we producing disciples through evangelism that results in baptisms and teaching that leads to obedience?

Tim, our example of an unnurtured new believer, seemed to grow spiritually. Inside, though, he was often a defeated Christian. When he tried to pray, his mind was easily distracted. Sporadic devotions produced few insights, and he almost gave up on Bible reading. Tim was under daily spiritual attack.

Tim became a convert but not a disciple—yet his church assumed that they had fulfilled their responsibility. The goal in the second half of this chapter is to show that Tim's church, in failing to complete the Great Commission mandate to baptize *and* teach, set him up for defeat in the battles of spiritual warfare.

Satan's Opposition to the Great Commission

Because "making disciples" is the central aspect of fulfilling the Great Commission, it stands to reason that Satan would want to scheme against churches that seek to produce disciples. Consider again Tim's story as we seek to understand Satan's schemes against believers who aren't fully discipled.

Why did Satan attack Tim? Tim was at age twenty a newborn believer, but he was still a baby in Christ (1 Cor. 3:1). We might think that Tim was not a threat to Satan at that stage of his spiritual journey, but just the opposite is true for at least two reasons. First, Tim was excited about his new faith in Christ. He sensed a new purpose for living and felt genuinely loved for the first time. He could pray when he had a problem, and he believed in faith that God heard him. The Bible was fresh and alive in those early days. Tim told everyone he met about Christ–and that enthusiasm itself made him a threat to the Enemy.

Second, Tim not only told everyone about Christ, but he also still knew unsaved people. He didn't need to search for someone to evangelize. Family members, neighbors, co-workers, and friends who did not know the Lord surrounded him. Even before he understood the Great Commission, he was doing the evangelism component. In response, Satan fired his arrows at the young believer (see Eph. 6:16). The Enemy always fights against believers who obey the Great Commission.

The Enemy often strikes at new believers with the same temptations they faced before they became Christians. Tim had assumed that when he became a believer, he would no longer struggle with those sin issues. He believed that he would always experience spiritual victory. Some believers even told him that they had conquered all of their sin. So he was surprised when old temptations returned. He still fought the desire to listen when co-workers told immoral jokes. Lustful thoughts still crept in when he saw young women. Curses were still a first emotional response when something went wrong. Sometimes Tim found himself committing the same sins he had committed before he became a Christian.

Through these failures, Satan raised doubts about his conversion. Because Tim still faced and often fell to temptation, he wondered whether his conversion was genuine. He also had seen others respond to Christ with tears and great emotion—but he had experienced neither in his own conversion. Unwilling to admit his confusion, Tim struggled with his doubts in silence and compensated by energetic church involvement. *Maybe if I do a lot in the church, I will prove that I'm a Christian.* And leaders who failed to disciple him readily took advantage of Tim's willingness to serve. They called on him to teach even before he had begun to learn.

Satan also capitalized on Tim's loneliness as a new believer. When Tim became a Christian, he knew he could no longer live as he had. He stopped having sexual intercourse with his girlfriend. The bars and the late-night parties with work buddies were no longer options. When Tim shared Christ with his friends, they became uncomfortable and began to avoid him. Tim's relationships changed drastically.

But in the body of Christ, it wasn't easy to develop new ties. Tim was involved, but he didn't feel entirely welcomed. Most people already had particular circles in which they invested themselves. As a new member, Tim felt uncomfortable taking the initiative to get to know longer-term members. Consequently, he felt alone—uneasy in his former world and uncomfortable in his new world of the church.

Do you see Satan's strategy? Young, excited, but untaught, converts under spiritual attack become defeated believers. They ultimately remain weak believers—even when they become leaders in our churches. Undiscipled leaders don't produce discipled warriors.

The Church's Proper Response

What, then, must the church do to counter Satan's strategy? Think back to the layout of Ephesians discussed in the last chapter.[4] Ephesians 1–3 are the theological chapters that form the foundation of a healthy church. Ephesians 4–6 are the application chapters, the rooftop of this church model.

Exhibit 2-2 The Message of Ephesians

1:1–3:21 Foundation of the Model	4:1–6:9 Application/Rooftop of the Model
Purpose Theology/beliefs: We are "in Christ."	**Purpose** Praxis/behavior: Christ in us must be lived out.
Focus The work of God: God in grace gives position and privileges to the believer.	**Focus** The walk of the Christian: Our position in Christ carries practical responsibilities.
Theme We are in Christ.	**Theme** Because we are in Christ, we must walk worthy of our calling.
Application Elected in Christ, we have been made alive, created for good works, given His power and authority, and united in His church.	**Application** From our position in Christ, we show humility, patience, and gentleness in the church, in our personal lives, in our families, and in work relationships.

Recognizing that all believers face "powers and principalities," Paul concludes with a summary and command to "put on the full armor of God" (Eph. 6:11–17). As a summary, the warfare imagery reminds the Ephesians that the God who chose them (Eph. 1:4) is the same God whose armor they can wear (6:11). God is our shield (Gen. 15:1; Ps. 28:7), and it is He who chose to wear the breastplate of righteousness and the helmet of salvation (Isa. 59:17). Christ Jesus is truth (John 14:6), and

God's Word is the only sword in battle (Eph. 6:17). Hence, the God of Ephesians 1–3 is the focus of 6:10–20.

As a call to action, Ephesians 6:10–20 emphasizes three commands:

1. Be strong (v. 10);
2. put on (v. 11); and
3. stand (vv. 11, 14).

By putting on the full armor of God, the Ephesians could resist the Enemy and stand against his schemes. Christ already ruled over the powers (Eph. 1:20–21; 3:10), but the believers were still to prepare and to fight diligently to experience that victory.

At the same time, the command to put on the armor should not be separated from the rest of what Paul wrote. A simple comparison shows clear connections between Ephesians 6:10–20 and the rest of the epistle:

- belt of "truth"
  - 1:13—"listening to the message of truth"
  - 4:15—"speaking the truth in love"
  - 4:21—"truth is in Jesus"
  - 4:24—"created in . . . holiness of the truth"
  - 4:25—"speak truth"
  - 5:9—"the fruit of the Light consists in all . . . truth"
- breastplate of "righteousness"
  - 4:24—"put on the new self . . . created in righteousness"
  - 5:9—"the fruit of the Light consists in all . . . righteousness"
- "gospel of peace"
  - 1:2—"Grace to you and peace"
  - 1:13—"the message of truth, the gospel of your salvation"

2:14–17—"He Himself is our peace . . . thus establishing peace . . . He came and preached peace"
3:6—"partakers of the promise in Christ Jesus through the gospel"
4:3—"preserve the unity of the Spirit in the bond of peace"

- shield of "faith"
  1:15—"having heard of the faith in the Lord Jesus"
  2:8—"by grace you have been saved through faith"
  3:12—"we have boldness and confident access through faith in Him"
  3:17—"Christ may dwell in your hearts through faith"
  4:5—"one faith"
  4:13—"until we all attain to the unity of the faith"
- helmet of "salvation"
  1:13—"the message of truth, the gospel of your salvation"
  2:5—"by grace you have been saved"
  2:8—"by grace you have been saved through faith"
  5:23—"He Himself being the Savior of the body"
- the sword of the Spirit, which is the "Word" of God
  5:26—"by the washing of water with the word"

Following this comparison, recognize that any legitimate attempts to address spiritual warfare cannot be separated from theological truths that focus on God and practical living that demands obedience. Ephesians 6:10–20 is not an addendum, but rather a challenge to those who are secure in God (chaps. 1–3) to live obediently (chaps. 4–6). They were to stand firm against the Enemy. We can add, then, a final section to our chart, as shown in Exhibit 2–3.

This approach to Ephesians corrects errors that frequently pervade contemporary spiritual warfare literature. These writings tend to focus on the Devil and neglect or even ignore

Exhibit 2-3 Summary of the Message of Eph. 6:10–20

Summary/Preparation: Theologically and positionally, our victory is secure in Christ. Practically, the spiritual battle continues. Prepare for and fight the spiritual battle by putting on and living out the armor of God.

God. Biblical spiritual warfare is *not* about knowing Satan–it is about so knowing God and walking with Him that we readily recognize the counterfeit offers of the Enemy.

Putting on the armor is about making disciples through teaching. The Ephesian believers needed to be taught to protect and arm themselves. Their spiritual battles were very real, and Paul wanted them to know how to defend themselves.

Paul's point, however, was not that the Ephesians were to discover new techniques and strategies for doing spiritual warfare. Rather, his point was that faithful Christian living is itself effective in undermining the Enemy. Indeed, New Testament scholar Peter O'Brien equates "putting on the armor" with Paul's command for the Ephesians to "put on the new self" (4:24).[5]

Defining the pieces of the armor will help in making this connection.[6] Wearing the armor is reflected in how we live as we fully imitate Christ (5:1):

- belt of truth

  Know Christ, who is the truth.

  Trust the truth of God's Word.

  Live truth by practicing honesty and integrity.
- breastplate of righteousness

  Be grateful for God's righteousness given to us.

  Live a life of holiness.

  Make righteous choices–imitate God.

- footcovering of the gospel of peace
  - Stand firm in faith.
  - Be willing and ready to share it.
  - Go where God calls.
  - Proclaim God's peace, even in the midst of spiritual battles.
- shield of faith
  - Know and trust God's promises.
  - Act in accordance with assurance that God will keep His promises.
- helmet of salvation
  - Having God's salvation, live in hope.
  - Know who you are in Christ.
  - Think differently than the world thinks.
- sword of the Spirit
  - Know God's Word.
  - Proclaim and teach it.

Having put on the armor, the believers were to pray:

- Keep alert in the battle, always in prayer.
- Pray for all believers.
- Pray for effective evangelism.

If putting on the armor is a lifestyle issue, how do new believers know they must wear it? How do they know what the armor is and how to fit it to their own lives? For each piece of armor, there are additional questions as well. For example, how do believers who want to wear the belt of truth know what truth is? How do they know how to study the Bible and incorporate scriptural truths into their lives? How does a believer who wants to carry the shield of faith know the promises of God? How does he make righteous choices, showing that he is wearing the breastplate of righteousness?

The answer to all of these questions is, of course, that the believer must be taught. Through teaching, believers learn to live effective Christian lives. Churches that fail to teach believers send them unarmed into the spiritual battle. They commit "spiritual child abuse" by allowing baby Christians to flounder in the war. At the end of the day, untaught believers such as Tim experience defeat in their spiritual walks.

Discipled Warriors and Healthy Church Growth

On the other hand, believers who are adequately taught and trained know how to stand against the Enemy by claiming the promises of God. They know how to extinguish Satan's darts through faith. They have learned how to pray effectively. They find guidance and strength in their devotions. They feel confident to share their faith at every opportunity. They are discipled warriors.

It is easy to see how producing discipled warriors relates to healthy church growth.

First, the command to put on the armor is corporate in nature. Certainly it is relevant for individuals, but we should recognize that Paul's commands in Ephesians 6:10–20 are addressed to the corporate body of Christ. Clinton Arnold concludes, "The whole church is involved in the process of arming. In fact, each believer is responsible for arming other believers."[7] Paul assumed that the process would take place within the context of the local church so that the healthy church stands obedient and united against the Enemy.

Second, discipled warriors walk courageously into the battle. Tommy is one of the most committed men of God that I know. As a young believer, he was privileged to have a mentor who discipled him. Tommy prays passionately and reads the Word of God fervently. His journal records of what God has taught him over the years would fill file cabinets. Tommy's faith, though, doesn't remain in his study. He is a soulwinner who reaches out to people who would frighten others. He is unafraid because he wears the armor of God as a genuine disciple.

Regrettably, Tommy is an exception instead of the norm. Healthy churches should be filled with believers like him.

Third, churches that fail to strategize discipleship are easy prey for the Enemy. Paul challenged the Ephesians to put on the armor of God "so that you will be able to stand firm against the schemes of the devil" (Eph. 6:11). Because Satan is a strategist, a schemer who knows how to attack, we must also strategize against his attacks.

Some congregations are easy targets simply because they have no direction, no purpose, and no united front. The Enemy easily wins some battles because his forces are more organized than are ours. Thus, legitimate attention to church growth principles, strategies, and purposes is much more than a quick-fix approach to growing numbers. Strategizing for growth is a necessary weapon in the spiritual war.

Application

Let's return to Tim's story one more time. Tim's life turned a corner when a brother in Christ began meeting regularly with him for Bible study. The two men developed a mentoring bond that gives Tim opportunities to study the Word, to ask questions, and to discuss spiritual matters. For the first time, he is experiencing growth in Christ. How sad that he spent many years in defeat before this perceptive Christian brother recognized his struggle.

Sadly, there are many undiscipled Tims. Their churches have failed to teach them, and no one has picked up the slack. When the Devil attacks, these undiscipled believers are wounded because they do not have the armor.

If you and other leaders are ready to change this pattern in your body, consider these possible starting points:

- Preach a sermon series on the Great Commission texts in the Bible.

- Conduct a study of the armor of God, focusing on the function of the passage in Ephesians.
- Enlist a focus group of church leaders to evaluate the church's internal (spiritual) growth. Consider conducting a survey to determine the members' commitment to Bible study, prayer, giving, etc.
- Make preliminary preparations to train members to do evangelism (see chap. 4 of this volume).
- Look for "Tims." They might be leading, but they have not been discipled. Establish an intensive discipleship program around their needs.
- Establish one-to-one teaching with an element of accountability for new converts.
- Conduct a survey to determine how aware members are of the purposes of the church. This will spot deficiencies that can be addressed in teaching and preaching.
- Organize a Christian reading group, and read biographies of great believers whose lives modeled victory in Christ. The *Heroes of the Faith* series (Barbour) and the *Library of Religious Biography* (Eerdmans) are such resources.
- Consider enlisting a church consultant to evaluate the overall strategy for evangelizing and teaching.
- If your church has no intentional strategy for disciple-making, work with leaders to develop one.
- Enlist a task force to contact inactive members, looking for those who have not been discipled. Invite these members to new learning opportunities.
- Begin considering strategies for helping members apply faith to every sphere of life. Use the next chapters to assist in this task.

For further study

Anderson, Neil T., and Charles Mylander. *Setting Your Church Free.* Ventura, Calif.: Regal, 1994.

Anderson, Neil T., and Timothy M. Warner. *The Beginner's Guide to Spiritual Warfare*. Ann Arbor, Mich.: Vine, 2000.

Arias, Mortimer, and Alan Johnson. *The Great Commission: Biblical Models for Evangelism*. Nashville: Abingdon, 1992.

Banks, William L. *In Search of the Great Commission.* Chicago: Moody, 1991.

Coleman, Robert. *The Master Plan of Discipleship*. Grand Rapids: Baker, 1998.

Dever, Mark. *Nine Marks of a Healthy Church.* Wheaton, Ill.: Crossway, 2000.

Gurnall, William. *The Christian in Complete Armour*. Edited and introduced by James S. Bell Jr. Chicago: Moody, 1994.

Hughes, Robert Don. *Satan's Whispers: Breaking the Lies that Bind.* Nashville: Broadman, 1992.

MacNair, Donald J. *The Practices of a Healthy Church: Biblical Strategies for Vibrant Church Life and Ministry.* Phillipsburg, N.J.: Presbyterian and Reformed, 1999.

Malphurs, Aubrey. *Advanced Strategic Planning: A New Model for Church and Ministry Leaders*. Grand Rapids: Baker, 1999.

Miller, Calvin. *Disarming the Darkness: A Guide to Spiritual Warfare.* Grand Rapids: Zondervan, 1998.

Spurgeon, Charles. *Spiritual Warfare in a Believer's Life*, comp. R. Hall. Lynnwood, Wash.: Emerald, 1993.

Stanley, Charles. *Overcoming the Enemy*. Nashville: Thomas Nelson, 1997.

Wiersbe, Warren W., comp. *Classic Sermons on Spiritual Warfare*. Grand Rapids: Kregel, 1992.

Notes

1. I am aware that most scholars do not view Mark 16:9–20 as part of the original text. Regardless of one's view on this issue, the Great Commission passage in this gospel clearly reflects other undisputed Great Commission texts in the Gospels.
2. Richard Longenecker, ed., *Patterns of Discipleship in the New Tes-*

tament (Grand Rapids: Eerdmans, 1996), 4. Longenecker indicates that some form of the word is used 246 times in these books.

3. Donald McGavran, *Understanding Church Growth* (Grand Rapids: Eerdmans, 1970), 15.
4. Though original, this chart is a compilation of several other charts. See Scott Moreau, *INTR 567: Spiritual Conflict* (Wheaton: A. Scott Moreau, 1994), 15:9; Daniel L. Akin, *Riches and Responsibilities: An Exposition of Ephesians* (Louisville: Daniel Akin, 1997); *The Open Bible*, expanded ed. (Nashville: Thomas Nelson, 1985), 1160–61.
5. Peter T. O'Brien, *The Letter to the Ephesians* (Grand Rapids: Eerdmans, 1999), 462.
6. The chart reflects insights from O'Brien, *Letter to the Ephesians*, 456–90; Andrew Lincoln, "Ephesians," vol. 42 of *Word Biblical Commentary* (Dallas: Word, 1990), 429–60; Klyne Snodgrass, *The NIV Application Commentary: Ephesians* (Grand Rapids: Zondervan, 1996), 334–46; Clinton Arnold, *Three Crucial Questions about Spiritual Warfare* (Grand Rapids: Baker, 1997), 42–43.
7. Clinton E. Arnold, *Powers of Darkness* (Downers Grove, Ill.: InterVarsity, 1992), 159.

CHAPTER 3

Discipled Warriors Exalting God

Matthew 22:36–37; Acts 2:43, 47

It was a typical Sunday morning in the Southern town. At First Church, a formal choir sang an anthem to a congregation primarily of people middle aged and older. Little had changed in this church's worship for decades. Anyone who suggested change was quickly accused of rejecting the church's tradition and heritage. Younger members tended to leave First Church and attend Second Church across town.

At Second Church, a praise band struck up the music precisely at 11 a.m. Excitement pervaded the auditorium as church members sang their choruses. Few noticed, though, the significant number who attended Sunday morning instructional programs but skipped worship because it was "too contemporary." Some attended "Sunday school" at Second, then joined the worship at First Church.

In another part of town, the worship leader at a charismatic assembly encouraged worshipers to use their praise to break Satan's power. "The Enemy always flees at the sound of praise!" he shouted over a raucous musical interlude. "Sing to the Lord, and the Devil will be bound in this place!" First Church people deride the charismatic church as unbiblical, and even some Second Church members tend to think the charismatics put too much emphasis on emotion.

So continues what one writer has referred to as "worship

wars."[1] More than one church has split over worship styles, and more than one pastor has lost his job when he tried to change the way worship has "always" been done.

Plenty has been said about worship wars among believers. What we will consider here is our call to worship God and the Devil's attempts to stifle that worship. This is a much more serious battle than the problems faced at the three churches of our illustration. The healthy church recognizes that this battle is real, keeps focusing on God, and trains discipled warriors who know how to worship.

Our Calling to Worship

The Bible opens with a simple statement that calls us to worship: "In the beginning God created the heavens and the earth" (Gen. 1:1). He who created the universe–including us–has a right to expect worship from us. *Worship is the proper response of the created to the Creator:* "Worthy are You, our Lord and our God, to receive glory and honor and power; for You created all things, and because of Your will they existed, and were created" (Rev. 4:11).

The final chapter of the Bible also includes a statement from Jesus that ought to evoke our worship: "Behold, I am coming quickly, and My reward is with Me, to render to every man according to what he has done. I am the Alpha and the Omega, the first and the last, the beginning and the end" (Rev. 22:12–13). He who is the eternal sovereign ruler over history, and who will be our final judge, deserves our worship. *Worship is the right response of the dependent to the Sovereign.*

Between these first and last chapters of the Bible is the story of a God who saves His own through the death of His Son (Rom. 5:8–10). The Bible records God's intervention on our behalf so that we might be reconciled to Him (2 Cor. 5:18–19). Such a gracious God certainly ought to receive our worship. *Worship is the necessary response from the redeemed to the Redeemer:*

"Worthy are You . . . for You were slain, and purchased for God with Your blood men from every tribe and tongue and people and nation" (Rev. 5:9).

God is the sovereign Creator and ultimate Judge, but He is also our loving Redeemer. When we truly recognize who He is, worship should be the result. The healthy church must, in fact, exalt God. We are to love Him with all of our being (Matt. 22:37–38), and awe and praise should characterize our relationship with Him (Acts 2:43, 47). Worship should be a *lifestyle* of submission and service, as the words used for *worship* in Scripture indicate:

- *shahah* (Heb.) means to bow or stoop before someone (e.g., Exod. 4:31).
- *avad* (Heb.) means to labor or do service (e.g., Exod. 3:12).
- *proskynein* (Gk.) means to prostrate oneself or to kiss the hand (e.g., John 4:24).
- *latreuein* (Gk.) means to do ministry or service (e.g., Rom. 12:1).

Christians badly miss the point if they understand "worship" as only a Sunday morning gathering designed to make us feel good about ourselves and about our religion. So do those who assume that worship is an evangelistic event directed toward exposing nonbelievers to the gospel. Worship, it seems, has become more about human beings than about God. How did the concept of worship become so distorted?

Ron Owens, musician and associate for *Experiencing God* author Henry Blackaby, believes that behind these misunderstandings is an Enemy who seeks to confuse God's people.[2] In fact, that Enemy has himself a distorted sense of worship.

While the Bible does not satisfy all of our curiosity about the origins and being of Satan, he may have rebelled against God as an angel identified as Lucifer or Daystar, seeking his own glory (Isa. 14:12–15; also Ezek. 28:1–19). His heart became proud

(Ezek. 28:17), and he proclaimed, "I will ascend to heaven; I will raise my throne above the stars of God. . . . I will make myself like the Most High" (Isa. 14:13–14). The created one sought to be worshiped over the Creator.

Since that day, attacks on believers have often centered on distorting genuine worship. Think about why Satan gives his attention to worship.

Primarily, worship is about God, and the one who rebelled against God does not want us to focus on Him. The reality is that the Enemy does not care if we gather for a worship service—as long as our attention is on everything but God. He allows us to build our altars, so long as we don't really pay honor to God there. This important subject will come up again below.

Worship also affects all that the church does. In our model of the healthy church, worship is one of six purposes of the church that is built on a theological foundation centered on God. Each of the purposes is equally important, but none of the other five exists apart from worship.

1. We *evangelize* so that all the world will be drawn to worship a holy and merciful God.
2. We *equip* believers so that their lives might give worthy praise in service.
3. We *edify* others through ministry intended to be a practical expression of praise and adoration.
4. We *encounter* God in prayer as One worthy to hear our praises and confessions, even as He responds to our petitions.
5. We *encourage* each other through fellowship as part of our mandate to honor Him with our lives and uphold His standards.

If our worship is awry, every other purpose in the church is affected. One reason Satan attacks worship is that the entire church is weakened when our worship is wrong. Jealous of God's praise and desiring to stop it, the Enemy schemes to attack worship. To some of those schemes we now turn.

Strategies of the Enemy

Genuine worship develops from a proper attitude of the heart. When we truly encounter Him and recognize Him for who He is, we can only cry out with Isaiah, "Woe is me, for I am ruined! Because I am a man of unclean lips" (Isa. 6:5). Hence, Satan's primary goal is to direct us away from God so that our worship is at least misdirected if not nonexistent.

The Enemy invites us to focus on ourselves, while genuine worship requires us to focus on God.

Both Matthew (4:1–11) and Luke (4:1–13) record that the Devil intentionally tempted Jesus early in His ministry. The first temptation was for Jesus to turn stones into bread. Hungry from weeks of fasting, surely Jesus had legitimate reason to focus on His own needs. Ultimately, Satan's goal was for Jesus to reject the Father and to worship him instead (Matt. 4:9, Luke 4:7). Jesus, though, kept His focus on the Father and chose to worship Him alone.

One of the Enemy's subtle ways to direct us away from genuine worship is to focus us on our own needs. In Exodus 32:1–10, Moses had been on the mountain so long that the people assumed that they no longer had a leader or a God to go before them. Unwilling to wait and concerned mostly about their own needs, they said to Aaron, "Come, make us a god who will go before us" (32:1). Focusing on themselves led them to idolatry when they worshiped a golden calf rather than the true God.

Even if we are not blatant idolaters like the Hebrews, we sometimes fall into the same trap. The Enemy directs our attention to ourselves and our own needs, worries, and concerns. When these concerns cloud our worship, we're dangerously close to making an idol of them.

How difficult it is to worship when your mind is on unpaid bills, your children are in trouble, or a job layoff is imminent. Is worship easy in the context of a loveless marriage or poor health? Such needs must be addressed, but we also must be able to set them aside to focus on God. Worship is about God, not us. The Enemy, however, wants us to focus so much on ourselves that we can attend an entire worship service and never really see God.

On this issue, the critics of "felt needs" preaching deserve to be heard. Addressing felt needs might be a legitimate means to attract the unchurched, but this approach to preaching is insufficient to foster genuine worship. A steady diet of human-centered messages furthers the Enemy's agenda to focus attention on ourselves. Consumers seldom become discipled warriors.

The Enemy offers the temporal, while genuine worship demands a focus on the eternal.

In his encounter with Jesus, the Devil offered Him all the kingdoms of the world. Think about the brashness of this temptation. The Devil believed that temporal kingdoms could lure the Son of God. He offered Him the world, trying to direct Jesus' attention away from the eternal plan of God—the cross.

Jesus' response was swift and forceful: "Go, Satan! For it is written, 'You shall worship the Lord your God, and serve Him only!" (Matt. 4:10). Jesus knew that obedience to the Father demanded His death. There was no shortcut to gaining the world. Genuine worship for Jesus meant radical obedience to the Father's eternal plan.

Satan does not have to offer us the world to steal our worship. He only directs our attention toward the temporary, so that the eternal seems insignificant. Our goals and plans become more important than what God wants. Spiritual growth becomes less important than climbing the corporate ladder. Jobs, education, relationships, homes, and other temporal issues overshadow God.

After studying the nature of the North American church and the lost people around it, Tom Clegg and Warren Bird concluded that lost people are still looking for spiritual answers, but they no longer look to the church.[3] Alternatives abound in New Age channelers, Internet chat rooms, Eastern mystical religions, and psychic hotlines. Is it possible that the problem is not that the alternative religions are so attractive but that the church no longer focuses on the eternal?

Evaluate the formal worship experiences of your congregation, asking a few penetrating questions. For example, "What happened today that directed worshipers from the temporary to the eternal?" "What are we doing to help believers develop a lifestyle of worship?" The Enemy has won a victory if your honest answer to either question is, "Nothing."

The Enemy offers power, while genuine worship results in brokenness.

The snake in the Garden of Eden offered Adam and Eve power that they had not known before: "In the day you eat from it [the tree], your eyes will be opened, and you will be like God, knowing good and evil" (Gen. 3:5). God was holding them back, the Enemy proposed, because He did not want them to be as powerful as He.

A similar offer of power echoed in the temptation of Jesus (Matt. 4:1–11). The Enemy tempted Him to misuse His power to make bread. He tempted Him to test God's concern and power by jumping from the temple. The Devil offered the power behind the kingdoms of the world, if only Christ would compromise.

If Satan offered that authority to Jesus, believing that even *He* might be susceptible to it, how much more might he try to attract us to power? Our wrestling match is against powers (Eph. 6:12) who want us to seek power for our own success and authority.

Believers succumb to the temptation of power even in the very context of what are supposed to be worshiping communities. Some people think that they should have control over what happens within the church. Power-hungry groups welcome some and reject others. They fear new efforts over which they might not have control. The pervasive attitude is, "This is our church, and we're in charge here."

Pastors and staff members are also vulnerable to this temptation of power. Sometimes we see one congregation as a stepping stone to larger, more important ministry offers. Unspoken dreams of an earthly kingdom drive us forward.

If church leaders and laypersons are jockeying for power and popularity, the worship service sometimes becomes only a showplace where "God is often being used to display man's talent rather than man's talent being used to display God."[4]

Contrast this competitive, arrogant spirit with the attitude of genuine worshipers. Abram fell on his face (Gen. 17:3). So did Joshua (Josh. 5:14), Ezekiel (Ezek. 1:28), and the magi (Matt. 2:11). Gideon bowed (Judg. 7:15), and the people of Ezra's day bowed low to worship the Lord with their faces to the ground (Neh. 8:6). The apostle John on the Isle of Patmos fell at Christ's feet like a dead man (Rev. 1:17). Isaiah immediately confessed his uncleanness (Isa. 6:5). Brokenness and dependence still mark those who truly know how to worship.

The Enemy encourages careless worship, while genuine worship requires that we worship God's way.

In Genesis 4, God rejected Cain's offering of worship (4:3–5). In Leviticus 10, God struck dead two sons of Aaron for offering "unauthorized fire" on the altar (vv. 1–3). Whatever the nature of these men's sins, they make the point abundantly clear that God expects His children to worship *His* way. Careless attention to the details of worship might bring the judgment of a God for whom worship is deadly serious.

Jesus taught that we must worship "in spirit and truth" (John 4:24). Genuine worshipers are born of the Spirit (John 3:5–6), brought to knowledge of God through Christ (John 14:6). In response, true worshipers have an attitude of dependence and integrity before God. Gratitude, confession, and holiness mark their worship. Only one with clean hands, a pure heart, and no deceit can stand in the holy place (Ps. 24:3–4).

On the other hand, prideful hearts negate offerings (Amos 4:4–5). Rituals mean little if our hearts are not broken and contrite (Ps. 51:16–17). In fact, careless observance of the Lord's Supper cost the lives of some in Corinth (1 Cor. 11:27–30).

Perhaps one example of what I consider "careless worship" might help here. In many churches, the worship service *ends* with a time of response when believers have an opportunity to "get right" with God. I affirm this response time, but if we make things right only at the end of the service, we are most ready to worship only *as we leave.* The service thus becomes more a preparation *for* worship than a time *of* worship.

How might worship change—and how might the Enemy be more threatened—if the church *gathered ready for worship*? How might worship change if we worship God's way?

The Enemy encourages division over worship, but genuine worship unites believers.

More than one writer has facetiously suggested that the first murder in the Bible occurred over a difference in worship styles (Cain and Abel—Gen. 4:1–8). Clearly, the issues of Genesis 4 were much more significant than worship style, but powerful emotions are associated with stylistic preferences, as in First Church and Second Church above.

Because disunity threatens the church's witness (John 17:20–23), the Enemy will exploit any disagreement to foster disunity. His schemes to divide are especially effective when he capitalizes on strong personal preferences such as worship style. No church genuinely worships if their focus is always on themselves and their own preferences.

I do believe that some worship "styles" are not conducive to biblical worship. Human-centered worship that lacks a focus on God and His preached Word hardly promotes biblical worship. My personal style preferences, however, do not allow me to assume that God cannot be worshiped through other styles.

I have worshiped in Russia, where the style tends to be liturgical and somewhat slow, in the Philippines with choruses and uplifted hands, and in Africa with upbeat, expressive singing that was *way too fast* for me. I have not always been comfortable with the style, but I never went away feeling that I had not worshiped God.

Learning to worship together prepares us for the day when the multitude in heaven includes people "from every nation and all tribes and peoples and tongues" (Rev. 7:9). Somehow, I suspect that the Enemy would not want us to experience that kind of worship on this side of eternity.

The Healthy Church Stands Armed

Worship is not optional for the healthy church. Because genuine worship affects all that the church does, the devil strives diligently to hinder the church's worship. Consider the following steps to a healthy church and arm your congregation against the Enemy's attacks on worship.

Focus on God.

We have already said that worship is about God. *It may surprise you to know that spiritual warfare is also about God, not about the Devil.* As a seventh-grader, I traveled with my classmates to Washington, D.C. There we watched behind a glass wall as United States government officials printed dollar bills. When one of our teachers asked about counterfeit money, our guide said, "We have people trained to recognize counterfeit. They spend most of their time examining real dollar bills. In fact, they spend so much time examining the real thing that they can pick out a fake when it comes through."

That is the way that we recognize the Devil, too. It is not by reading every book that talks about the Devil's schemes. It is not by searching out evil spirits. The primary task of the discipled warrior is *not* to know Satan well–it is to know God so intimately that Satan's counterfeit becomes obvious by contrast (see Exhibit 3-1).

God alone must be the focus of a church that wants to win spiritual battles, because it is *God's* armor that we wear (Eph. 6:11). Remember that He is our shield (Gen. 15:1; Ps. 28:7), and it is He who chose to wear the breastplate of righteousness

Exhibit 3-1 God and Satan

God is . . .	Satan is . . .
• Creator (Gen. 1:1)	• Destroyer (Rev. 9:11)
• Almighty (Gen. 17:1)	• Limited by God (Job 1:12)
• Truth (John 14:6)	• Father of Lies (John 8:44)
• Love (1 John 4:8)	• Hatred/Murderer (John 8:44)
• Righteousness (Jer. 23:6)	• Evil (Matt. 6:13)
• Our Advocate (1 John 2:1)	• Our Accuser (Rev. 12:10)
• Our Protection in temptation (1 Cor. 10:13)	• The Tempter (Matt. 4:3)
• Ultimate Judge (Rev. 20:11–15)	• Ultimately Judged by God (Rev. 20:1–3)

and the helmet of salvation (Isa. 59:17). He who calls us to wield the sword of the Spirit is the Word (John 1:1; Eph 6:17). Discipled warriors understand, as did David and Jehoshaphat, that the battles we face are His rather than ours (1 Sam. 17:45–47; 2 Chron. 20:15).

Focusing on God reminds us that worship is a *lifestyle* issue, not just a Sunday morning issue. As you build the theological foundation of your church, call the congregation to give their whole lives to God. The Enemy cannot stand against that kind of worship.

Keep the Word central.

Three times Satan tempted Jesus in the wilderness, and three times Jesus quoted God's Word in response (Matt. 4:1–11). Each time, the power of Satan was no match for the power of the divinely inspired Scripture.

The implications for the healthy church are important. First, we must be cautious about emphasizing the power of warfare *techniques* over the truth of Scripture. Popular strategies such as "binding Satan" and "naming demons" focus more on proclaiming power instead of proclaiming biblical truth. Warfare inherently involves power struggles, but the truth of God's Word ultimately sets people free (John 8:32).

Second, the proclamation of the gospel is itself an act of warfare against Satan's kingdom. Our primary weapon against the Enemy is the sword of God's Word (Eph. 6:17). The Word of God is alive, and we have God's promise that it "will not return to Me empty, Without accomplishing what I desire, And without succeeding in the matter for which I sent it" (Isa. 55:11). It is no surprise, then, that Paul gave this explicit and challenging command to Timothy: "preach the word" (2 Tim. 4:2). The Enemy is dislodged when the Word is proclaimed.

Our researchers at the Billy Graham School of Missions, Evangelism and Church Growth conducted a comparative study showing that pastors of evangelistic churches spend *five times* more time in sermon preparation than do pastors of non-evangelistic churches (ten hours to two hours for each sermon).[5] Do you suppose that there is a reason why these churches are effective evangelistically? Pastors who devote themselves to the study and teaching of God's Word train discipled warriors and grow healthy churches.

Teach members to worship.

I never attended church before the day I became a Christian at age thirteen. Seven years later, I began my first pastorate. Fourteen years after that, a seminary professor challenged me to study the topic of worship. That study, to my recollection, was the first time that I had genuinely examined the subject. I had been a Christian for over twenty years, had pastored churches for fourteen years, and had led hundreds of worship services—but I had never been challenged to think in depth about what we were doing. I doubt that I am unique in that confession. When I did look carefully at worship, I learned some truths:

- Worship is about God.
- We don't invite God into our worship services; rather, God invites us into His presence.
- Holiness is not optional for the worshiper.
- Genuine worship changes people.
- Worship is not always defined or described easily. There is a mystery to worship.
- More than one worship style is modeled in the Bible.
- Heaven is about worshiping God forever.

If you want your church to be healthy, *teach them a biblical theology of worship*. Examine, for example, worship in the book of Revelation. Study Old Testament passages on worship regulations (e.g., the book of Leviticus). Reflect on the Psalms, the hymnal of the Israelites. Review what Jesus taught about worshiping in spirit and truth (John 4:24). Study other New Testament passages on worship order and structure (e.g., 1 Cor. 11:23–34). Teach your church about worship in the Bible if you want them to worship.

Teach the church about holy living. It is dangerous to be unholy in the presence of a holy God (Heb. 10:31). In fact, it may well be wrong to call ourselves a church if we are not characterized by holiness.

The people of God are to be holy because He is holy (Lev. 11:44). The church is a chosen people, but that chosenness demands that we stand against sin and stand for good works (1 Peter 2:9–12). The healthy church that wants to conquer the Enemy will call her members to holiness; and in that holiness, they will best worship.

Teach church members to worship in their homes. Ideally, worship begins in the home. Parents are to raise their children "in the discipline and instruction of the Lord" (Eph. 6:4), taking advantage of all opportunities to teach them about God (Deut. 6:7–9). Families who read the Bible together, pray together, and praise God together will contribute much toward worship in a healthy church.

My wife teaches a first-and-second-grade Sunday school class. She tells me that it is usually easy to know which class members live in homes where family worship occurs. These children know the Bible stories better. They know how to find passages in their Bibles. They are usually more willing to pray aloud. They tend to be more outreach-oriented, always bringing their friends to church. Hymns and choruses are usually more familiar to them. These children are being prepared to be discipled warriors before they ever come to church.

Teach the church about worship around the world. Churches with a global focus tend to be less self-centered and more willing to recognize that not everyone worships the same way. Invite missionaries to speak about different cultures. Ask international believers in your community to talk about worship in their homelands. Use missions videos to expose your church to other worship styles.

The Enemy wants to create division in the church over worship styles. Take the initiative to stop him before he ever gets a foothold—guide your church to appreciate the value of other styles. (By the way, this approach may also interest your church in missions, helping you to fulfill another of the church's purposes.)

Excursus–What about "Warfare Worship"?

Second Chronicles 20:14–23 describes the defeat of an enemy king through prayer and praise, rather than through armed conflict. The armies of Jehoshaphat stood against the invading armies of the Moabites and the Ammonites. The king's divinely given battle plans were odd, though. He was to send the choir in front of the army, praising God for His lovingkindness. As the choir sang, God set the ambush that would eventually bring the defeat of the enemies. The army only watched.

Some contend that praise and worship honors God and also makes "the devil shut up."[6] Much like the worship leader described in the opening paragraphs of this chapter, they believe that praise "binds" the devil. How should we respond to this understanding of worship?

A case can be made that praise does, in fact, counter the work of God's enemies. God used singing and praise in 2 Chronicles 20 to defeat the armies aligned against His people. Scholars such as Wayne Grudem also recognize the power of worship: "When God's people offer him worship today, we may expect that the Lord will battle against demonic forces that oppose the gospel and cause them to flee."[7]

What is not so evident, however, is that God's people are to praise and worship Him *so that* the Enemy will be defeated—and some practice warfare worship from this position.

> The seminar was about to come to a close when a woman came forward and requested prayer. . . . [The ministers] prayed and prayed, and there was no breakthrough. . . . All of a sudden, the head of the organization sent for a worshiper to come forward. This worshiper began to lead the group in intercessory praise—or praise warfare, as some call it. I went to the piano, and we began a type of warfare that is becoming quite frequent in prayer groups today—*warring against the works of Satan by worshiping the Lord*. . . . The women in the seminar stood to their feet. They sang; they clapped; they shouted; until suddenly the woman for whom they were praying began to weep and relate that the oppression had completely left her mind.[8]

This kind of warfare worship implies that on occasion believers should worship *in order to* break Satan's power. Worship initiated for that purpose misses the point. Effective spiritual warfare might be the *by-product* of worship, but it is not the *purpose* of worship. Discipled warriors worship God because of who He is, and that very focus on God weakens the Enemy's hold.

Application

In the fall of 2001, the United States stood on the brink of war with Afghanistan. News commentators around the country debated how long a war might last. Recurrently, we were reminded of the ten-year war that the Soviet Union had fought, and ultimately lost, in the same country. The Afghans would not succumb as quickly as had the Iraqis in the Persian Gulf War, we were told. They had withstood the superpower of the USSR, so we should prepare for a long battle against a fierce opponent.

Yet, in only a few months the basic power structure of the enemy government had been removed.

There were several reasons why so many military and news commentators had been mistaken in their projections. One was particularly obvious. Analysts assumed the potential strength of the Afghans on the basis of their strength against a different enemy (the Soviet Union). Indeed, the Afghan military had been effective against the USSR, but now the enemy was the United States, impassioned and solidly united by a shocking attack on their own country. That reality made all the difference.

My point is not to end this chapter with patriotic flag-waving. Rather, I want to show that an enemy who is strong against one force may not be so strong against another. It is not always correct to assume that a once-victorious force will always put up a good battle against every enemy.

We are in a spiritual war against a very real enemy who wields very real power. The history of the church is littered with stories of people who have lost this battle. The evil in our world today shows us that the battle is still raging. It seems at times that the Devil is winning. And, if we evaluate his strength just against human beings, we might assume that he will win in the end.

However . . . his battle is ultimately against a God who is omnipotent. The Enemy may at times win over us, but he will not win over God. Against humanity, he has power. Against God, he is nothing. God has already disarmed him through the cross (Col. 2:15), and he will finally bind him in the abyss (Rev. 20:1–3).

This God is worthy of worship. The following suggestions will help you as you lead your church to worship Him.

- Lead a study of texts about worship, perhaps starting with Isaiah 6.
- Preach a sermon series about worship in the book of Revelation.
- Introduce worship styles from around the world.
- Enlist a worship prayer team to pray that God will be

glorified in each worship service. Members can take turns praying throughout each service.

- Conduct a seminar on family worship.
- Write family devotions keyed to worship each week.
- Enlist laypersons to help conduct worship services in workplaces where permitted. This can begin in local hospitals, jails, and nursing homes, but some businesses might also permit lunchtime worship.
- Form a worship evaluation committee to offer suggestions for improving the focus on God in worship.
- Teach the significance of singing in worship and perhaps lead a special study from the Psalms just for those involved in music ministry.
- Send members to visit other churches where worship appears to be effective. Learn from other congregations, while following God's leading for your unique context.
- As church leaders, take time off to revitalize your own spiritual walk at worship conferences.
- Preach a sermon series on the attributes of God. Show why God is worthy of worship.
- Evaluate the order and outcome of worship services. Is the focus on God or on the people who lead?
- Encourage the church to worship God *daily* so that they are prepared to come together in corporate worship on the Lord's Day.

For further study

Basden, Paul. *The Worship Maze.* Downers Grove, Ill.: InterVarsity, 1999.

Coleman, Robert. *Songs of Heaven.* Tarrytown, N.Y.: Revell, 1982.

Cornwall, Judson. *Worship as Jesus Taught It.* Tulsa: Victory House, 1987.

Dawn, Marva. *A Royal "Waste" of Time: The Splendor of Worshiping God and Being Church for the World.* Grand Rapids: Eerdmans, 1999.

——. *Reaching Out Without Dumbing Down.* Grand Rapids: Eerdmans, 1995.

Frame, John M. *Contemporary Worship Music: A Biblical Defense.* Phillipsburg, N.J.: Presbyterian and Reformed, 1997.

——. *Worship in Spirit and Truth.* Phillipsburg, N.J.: Presbyterian and Reformed, 1996.

Martin, Ralph. *Worship in the Early Church.* Repr. ed., Grand Rapids: Eerdmans, 1995.

Morgenthaler, Sally. *Worship Evangelism.* Grand Rapids: Zondervan, 1995.

Owens, Ron. *Return to Worship.* Nashville: Broadman & Holman, 1999.

Peterson, David. *Engaging with God: A Biblical Theology of Worship.* Grand Rapids: Eerdmans, 1992.

Segler, Franklin M. *Christian Worship.* Nashville: Broadman & Holman, 1996.

Tozer, A. W. *Whatever Happened to Worship?* Camp Hill, Pa.: Christian Publications, 1985.

Webber, Robert. *Worship Old and New.* Grand Rapids: Zondervan, 1994.

Wenz, Robert. *Room for God?* Grand Rapids: Baker, 1994.

Notes

1. Elmer Towns, *Putting an End to Worship Wars* (Nashville: Broadman & Holman, 1997).
2. Ron Owens, *Return to Worship: A God-Centered Approach* (Nashville: Broadman & Holman, 1999).
3. Tom Clegg and Warren Bird, *Lost in America* (Loveland, Col.: Group, 2001), 40–41.
4. Owens, *Return to Worship,* 54.
5. Thom S. Rainer, *High Expectations* (Nashville: Broadman & Holman, 1999), 75–76. See also Rainer, *Effective Evangelistic Churches* (Nashville: Broadman & Holman, 1995).
6. Terry Law, *Power of Praise and Worship* (Tulsa: Victory House, 1985), 146.

7. Wayne Grudem, *Systematic Theology: An Introduction to Biblical Doctrine* (Grand Rapids: Zondervan, 1994), 1009.
8. Cindy Jacobs, *Possessing the Gates* (Grand Rapids: Chosen, 1991), 172–73; emphasis added.

CHAPTER 4

Discipled Warriors Evangelizing the World

Matthew 28:18–20; Acts 2:41, 47

Sometimes success in evangelism seems almost impossible. Alicia tried for years to win her friend Christie to the Lord. She told her about God's love, but Christie said she didn't need God's love. Alicia spoke about God's forgiveness, but her friend said she was good enough to be acceptable to God. Christie said that she didn't believe in hell anyway. In the end, Alicia gave up, discouraged that God wasn't answering her prayers in the way she wanted. She and Christie went their separate ways.

Have you ever been in that situation? The task of evangelism is not easy—that shouldn't surprise us. Evangelism is about reaching out to people who are caught in the Devil's snare. *Evangelism is itself a spiritual battle, as we take the gospel of light into the kingdom of darkness.* The healthy church that is ready to expand its efforts of evangelism had better be prepared to face spiritual warfare.

Our Calling to Evangelize the World

Jesus' disciples went from town to town at His command, telling others about their Lord (Mark 6:7–13). The early church followed suit, preaching Jesus in homes and the temple (Acts 5:41–42). The New Testament church *lived* evangelism. They took seriously Jesus' command to go, to baptize, and to teach

(Matt. 28:18–20). To reach the world, they proclaimed the Word and did missions. They preached in Jerusalem (Acts 2–7), in Judea and Samaria (8–12), and to the ends of the earth (13–28). Thousands believed (2:41, 4:4); many were healed (5:16); and entire people groups heard the gospel (8:4–17). What their enemies said of Paul and Silas, that they "turned the world upside down" (17:6 KJV), might also have been applied to other early Christians.

The success of the early church was not without battles. Disciples were imprisoned (Acts 4:1–3; 5:17–18). Satan led Ananias and Sapphira to bring deception into the church (5:1–11). Grumbling among the Greek widows hindered the fellowship with ethnic tensions (6:1). Stephen was martyred (7). Saul ravaged the church with persecution (8:3). Demons were encountered (5:16; 8:5–8; 16:16–21; 19:11–12, 13–17). The believers faced opposition on several fronts as their enemies tried to shut down the young church. Nevertheless, they moved forward, preaching to the masses (e.g., Acts 4:5–12; 8:4–8; 22:1–21) and to individuals (8:26–39; 16:27–34). They simply did not give up.

Our calling remains the same—to preach the gospel to the world in spite of any opposition that we might face (Matt. 28:18–20). We should expect opposition if we choose to be a healthy church committed to evangelizing the world.

Strategies of the Enemy

Adolf Hitler and his strategists conducted a varied campaign to gain control of Europe. German soldiers invaded Austria in 1938 and Czechoslovakia and Poland in 1939. In 1940, Hitler's forces attacked Denmark, Norway, France, Belgium, Holland, and Luxembourg. In each case, the aggressor was Germany, but the place and strategy of attack differed. That's the way that Satan and his forces battle against evangelism. Satan is always the Enemy, but he attacks on several fronts with different strategies. On one front, Satan and his demons work to keep nonbelievers spiritually blind. On another front, they seek to discourage and defeat individual believers who want to be witnesses for Christ. On still another, the Enemy battles against the corporate church to keep the body of Christ from reaching out.

Front 1: The Enemy blinds unbelievers to the gospel.

The apostle Paul told the Corinthian believers that "the god of this age has blinded the minds of unbelievers" (2 Cor. 4:3-4 NIV). The "god of this age" is Satan, who is also called the "prince of this world" (John 16:11 NIV) and the "ruler of the kingdom of the air" (Eph. 2:2 NIV). Nonbelievers are held under his dominion (Acts 26:18) in the "domain of darkness" (Col. 1:13). Consider how Satan keeps unbelievers in this darkness. Though he probably has multiple strategies, three are most obvious.

Satan blinds people by the lure of sin. Let's be honest–we sin because we are sinful by nature (Rom. 5:12; Eph. 2:3), but we also sin because we like it. The fruit on the tree looks good, and we willingly and enthusiastically bite into it.

Think about how Satan entices us into sin. In your mind, draw a "sin line" to divide the room in which you are reading. On one side of the line, you are not in sin. On the other side, you are in sin (see Exhibit 4–1).

Exhibit 4-1 The Sin Line

Not in sin	In sin

Just how close do we come to this "sin line" when we face temptation? In many cases, we crowd the line, trying to wring as much fun out of the temptation as we can. We put ourselves in vulnerable situations, hoping that we won't miss anything—yet all the while also hoping that we won't give in. Then we wonder why we failed to stand against Satan.

Why do we so easily cross the sin line, even when we know we're headed in the wrong direction? The Enemy always makes sin look inviting enough that we ignore the long-term consequences of our actions.

For instance, Jacob lied to gain an immediate blessing, ignoring the potential results in his family (Gen. 27:30–41). David was enticed by Bathsheba's beauty (2 Sam. 11:1–5), and he apparently thought little about the consequences of adultery. Ananias and Sapphira were caught because they wanted to look like self-sacrificing Barnabas without actually giving everything to God. They seemed unconcerned about the repercussions of their spiritual pride and grasping greed upon the early church (Acts 5:1–11). When the sin looks inviting, we seldom stop at the sin line.

These line-crossers were God's people. We have no reason to believe that Ananias and Sapphira were unsaved. So what about unbelievers, who are without *any* ultimate spiritual understanding (Rom. 3:11)? Condemned, their darkness becomes darker as they experience pleasure from their sin (John 3:18–20). Why should they want to turn from something they enjoy? In fact, they might consider God to be a killjoy because He only wants to take away their fun. Blinded by the Enemy through the lure of sin, they are naturally resistant to the gospel.

Satan blinds people by giving them lies to believe. Everybody believes something in the spiritual realm, even if we don't recognize our beliefs as such. Even an atheist believes *something*—that is, that there is no God. The Enemy wants people to believe something, as long as that "something" is a lie that he's given them.

The Devil is, in fact, the "father of lies" (John 8:44). He lied to Adam and Eve about their impending death as judgment against their sin (Gen. 3:4), and he has enticed people with lies since that day. Listen to some of the other lies that people believe today:

- "God is a loving God who wouldn't allow anyone to go to hell."
- "You'll always have tomorrow to follow God. Enjoy yourself today."
- "There are many routes to God. Just choose the one that best fits you."
- "Jesus was just a man. He wasn't God."
- "The Bible isn't really the Word of God."

Think back to Alicia's friend Christie in the opening illustration of this chapter. Christie rejected the gospel, choosing instead to believe that she was good enough for God to accept her. She also denied the reality of hell. The Enemy had snared her with lies.

Satan's lies are almost always built upon humanity's natural self-centeredness. If I can choose my own route to God, then I set myself up as God. If I believe that God is so loving that He would not allow anyone to go to hell, I must be safe from eternal damnation. If the Bible is not the Word of God anyway, then I need not worry about its teachings—I may live my life as I choose. The Enemy's lies thus draw non-believers further into their self-centeredness and sin that separate them from God.

Unfortunately, false teachers in the church are sometimes the source of these lies. Satan is so deceptive that he disguises himself as an angel of light, served by false teachers who disguise themselves as ministers of righteousness (2 Cor. 11:13–15). Do you see more clearly why a strong theological foundation is essential in a healthy church that encounters spiritual warfare?

The Enemy snatches the Word away when non-believers hear. Ken attended the first church I pastored for about four months.

Each Sunday during the first two months he attended, he wept through the services. Every week, I assumed that he would speak with someone about his desire to follow Christ.

With each succeeding month, though, Ken grew less responsive. He was less open to speaking about Christ. His emotions were less stirred. You could just watch as his heart hardened and the Enemy snatched the Word from him each week. Eventually, Ken never returned to the church.

Jesus warned us that such things would happen. The evil one will take away the Word from nonbelievers, so that "they will not believe and be saved" (Luke 8:4–15). When the Word takes no root in a person's life, the unbeliever remains blinded.

Front 2: The Enemy seeks to discourage and defeat believers.

Think about the implications of Satan's schemes to keep unbelievers blinded to the gospel. Evangelism demands that we take the gospel to people who are often enjoying their sin, while they are hanging on to spiritual lies that protect them. We are called to take the gospel of light to people who have been so deceived that they don't even know that they are in darkness. Clearly, God must intervene to help people recognize their darkness.

God has chosen to use us as His instruments of light in a world of darkness. We are to be the light of the world, letting our works shine so that God is glorified (Matt. 5:14–16). As followers of Jesus, we are to reflect His light (John 8:12).

If God wants to use us as His light, does it not make sense that the Enemy wants to extinguish that light? He doesn't want us to be effective witnesses for Christ. After all, what nonbeliever will listen to a believer whose life lacks victory?

Satan attacks believers with continual temptations to sin. Sometimes believers are discouraged by recurrent struggles with sin. Temptation occurs again and again, and it seems like we will never find victory. Defeat leads to discouragement, and discouragement leads to less resolve to fight the next temptation. The cycle becomes a vicious pattern of defeat:

Exhibit 4-2 The Pattern of Defeat

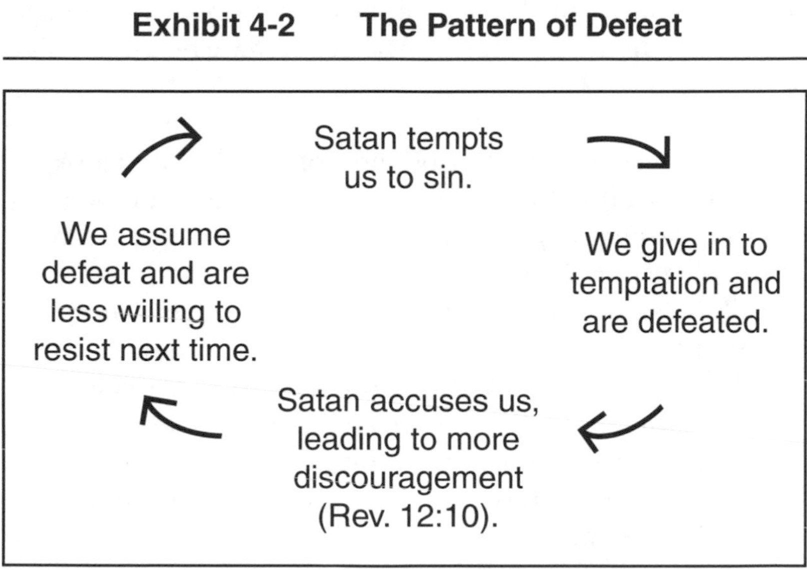

In rapid fashion, Peter faced this kind of battle after Jesus was arrested. Three times, he denied knowing Jesus (Matt. 26:69–75). He denied his relationship with Christ, then later denied Him "with an oath," and finally denied Him with cursing and swearing. Peter's willingness to stand for Christ must have weakened considerably with each succeeding denial. He listened to the Enemy's voice and temporarily lost his witness.

This process of defeat is seldom as rapid for us as it was for Peter. Our struggle with particular sins is usually longer term, but the effect on our witness is still destructive. Believers who constantly wrestle with and lose battles in temptation offer little hope to a hurting world.

Satan fosters discouragement even among faithful believers. Dedicated, faithful believers are also the target of the Enemy's attacks. Job was a blameless, upright man, yet Satan attacked him in violent ways (Job 1:1, 13–19). Even Job's wife suggested that he just curse God and die (2:9).

Job remained faithful under the Devil's attacks, but we aren't always as consistent. We are often easily prey to discouragement when the Enemy attacks. Maybe you have heard this kind of message:

> You've been faithful to God most of your life, and look what it's brought you. You still can't pay your bills. You're still struggling with that same sin. You've been reading your Bible and praying, but your children are still breaking your heart. Your spouse blames you for all of the problems. To top it all off, your church–to which you go for comfort and support–is in chaos. The pastor has fallen morally, and even other believers are hurting you. What's the point of your Christianity if this is all you get out of it? Don't you doubt God's care and concern?

Satan knows that discouraged believers usually make few efforts to tell others about Jesus. In the end, the believer's light is only a flickering candle that makes little difference to blinded unbelievers.

Let's be sure to be clear here. Unbelievers are fully accountable to God for their disobedience. They are separated from Him by their nature and by their actions (Rom. 3:23; Eph. 2:1–3). Nevertheless, the Devil doesn't sit idly by as unbelievers reject God. He works to keep their minds blinded by luring them into sin, by giving them lies to believe, by snatching away the Word, and by defeating believers who are called to be God's witnesses. Satan fights hard to keep unbelievers in darkness.

Front 3: The Enemy encourages inwardly focused churches.

As you recall, the healthy church model presented in this book includes a cross at the top, indicating the church's responsibility to take the gospel *to the world*. God is a missions-minded God who took the initiative to go to a lost world, and He expects us to be willing to do the same (Matt. 28:18–20).

Christians must, writes one missions professor, imitate God's "commitment to the salvation of all peoples and seek to complete in their own lives the task of global evangelization, which he himself began and commissioned them to continue."[1]

Cross-cultural missionaries face intense spiritual battles in the most anti-Christian regions of darkness. One missionary I know serves "under the radar" in a Muslim country. Every day, she places her safety on the line by seeking opportunities to tell others about Jesus. Those who accept the Lord usually are disowned by their families and can be imprisoned by the government. In the midst of such hatred, evangelist and convert alike battle discouragement, loneliness, and fear.

The Enemy works daily to defeat those who have invaded the darkness, but believers and churches that are unconcerned about missions do not alarm him. In fact, he prefers that self-centered and inward-focused churches pay little attention to the needs of the 1.6 billion people who have never heard the gospel.[2] The healthy church that wants to win the battles of spiritual warfare must think and minister globally. While not all believers are called to international missions, we are all expected to support efforts to fulfill the Great Commission. Anything less than a global focus plays into the Devil's strategy to keep unbelievers blinded.

Lakeview Baptist Church in Auburn, Alabama, has captured this missionary spirit. Led by Pastor Al Jackson, whose own heart beats for international missions, this church conducts a missions emphasis week, promotes several missions offerings, and sponsors mission trips every year. More than *forty* singles or couples from Lakeview now serve on mission fields around the world. At the same time, the church reaches hundreds of unbelievers for Christ in their own city annually. Outwardly focused and committed to evangelism and missions, this church is intentionally taking the gospel into the darkness. Such a church is likely to face spiritual battles, so Lakeview has a minister of prayer whose job is to challenge the church to stay on their knees.

The Healthy Church Stands Armed

During times of war, the work of gathering intelligence about the enemy is critical. Undercover agents and electronic surveillance look for significant bits of information about the enemy's plans. With such knowledge, military forces can counter the strategy before it's carried out. On the spiritual battlefield, we are not ignorant of the Enemy's schemes (2 Cor. 2:11). In His Word, God has given enough information about the Enemy's strategy against evangelism that we should be able to prepare our response.

Arm believers through biblical discipling.

Why do some believers catch fire for evangelism but then fizzle? Part of the reason is that we train believers to evangelize, but we don't train them to put on the armor of God (Eph. 6:11–18). When the Enemy attacks them *because* they have chosen to evangelize, they are not prepared. Unarmed evangelists are vulnerable to the Enemy's messages:

- "You're not good enough to be a witness for God. What about your own sin? How can you talk about victory when you're living in defeat?"

- "What will you do when they ask you biblical questions that you can't answer? Don't take that risk."
- "If you tell them they're lost, you will lose their friendship. You don't really want that to happen, do you?"
- "You've tried to witness to other people, and nobody's been saved yet. Why do you keep wasting your time?"

Believers who haven't been discipled become discouraged when the Enemy attacks. Discouraged warriors don't last long in the war.

In contrast, the church that is making disciples will prepare evangelistic believers for the Enemy's attacks. These believers will know how to counter Satan's lies to nonbelievers with the truth of the Word (see Exhibit 4-3). Their hope will remain strong because they have learned how to apply the promises of God. They will be confident enough to give a solid defense for their faith. They will know how to pray effectively. They will not battle alone, for they understand the power of Christian fellowship.

Remember Tim in chapter 2? As a new believer, he was excited to tell his friends about his new faith in Jesus. He could not wait to tell the good news he had experienced. Quickly, the attacks started. Temptations returned. Doubts arose. Loneliness set in. And Tim, who was not discipled to put on the armor of God, lost his enthusiasm. Evangelism was no longer part of Tim's life.

You, on the other hand, can help your church be healthy enough to overcome the Enemy by encouraging systematic disciplemaking. Discipled members are ready to face the battles that accompany evangelism. As pastor or leader, arm your Tims to maintain their passion for telling the good news.

Exhibit 4-3 Countering Satan's Lies

Lie . . .	Truth . . .
"You're good enough. God will accept you."	Isa. 64:6; Mark 10:18
"You'll always have tomorrow to follow God."	Prov. 27:1; Luke 12:16–21; Heb. 9:27
"There are many paths to God."	John 14:6; Acts 4:12
"God is so loving that He would never judge you."	2 Cor. 5:10
"Hell isn't a real place anyway."	Luke 16:19–31; Rev. 20:11–15

Proclaim good news.

The English word *evangelism* is a transliteration of the Greek word *euangelion*, meaning "good news; gospel." The prefix *eu* means "good," as in "euphoria" (a good feeling) and "euphemism" (a good or pleasant word). The rest of *euangelion* is the root for our word *angel*. The term has to do with news or a message. An angel is God's messenger. To evangelize is to be a messenger of good news.

Biblical evangelism assumes that we have a specific message of good news to proclaim. That message is clear: "Having been justified by faith, we have peace with God through our Lord Jesus Christ. . . . But God demonstrates His own love toward us, in that while we were yet sinners, Christ died for us. Much more then, having now been justified by His blood, we shall be saved from the wrath of God through Him" (Rom. 5:1, 8–9).

The gospel is about God's coming to us in Christ, dying for us on Calvary, saving us through His blood, living in us through

His Spirit, and ultimately welcoming us into heaven. No wonder the angel in Bethlehem said to the shepherds, "Behold, I bring you good news [*euangelizō*, "I preach good news"] of great joy which will be for all the people; for today in the city of David there has been born for you a Savior, who is Christ the Lord" (Luke 2:10–11).

Biblical evangelism is about telling that good news. *Anything less than the telling of this good news is not evangelism* (hence, this purpose in our model is evangelizing the world through *proclamation* and missions). The Enemy is not alarmed when we preach good messages, tell comforting stories, and affirm each other—as long as we never tell the good news of Jesus, the Son of God.

In *Lord Foulgrin's Letters*, a senior demon (Foulgrin) is supervising a junior demon (Squaltaint) as he seeks to deceive and mislead a human being named Fletcher. Listen to Foulgrin's directions concerning Fletcher's evangelistic efforts:

> Since it's what the Enemy [God] uses to change vermin destinations from hell to heaven, obviously you must keep Fletcher from evangelism. But don't bother trying to convince him it's bad to evangelize. Let him think it's good, admirable. *Just as long as he doesn't actually do it*. . . . Let Fletcher be a "good example" until he's blue in the face—as long as he doesn't explain the forbidden message. Let him talk with them about anything and everything but what the Enemy has done and what it means to be His follower.[3]

Counter this strategy by leading your church to proclaim the gospel intentionally and specifically. Teach them the gospel (thus strengthening the theological foundation of your church), and send them out. Proclaim the truth to undermine the Enemy's lies that hold nonbelievers in bondage. That truth that will set people free (John 8:32).

Train members to share.

A study sponsored by the Billy Graham organization discovered that *fear* is the leading obstacle to believers' witnessing.[4] Another study revealed these reasons for unwillingness to share:[5]

- 62 percent are afraid of embarrassment;
- 51 percent do not know what to say;
- 45 percent do not know the answers to questions they might be asked;
- 32 percent simply rarely think about doing evangelism;
- 27 percent say they have not found any "style" with which they are comfortable;
- 24 percent are shy or insensitive to others; and
- 5 percent do not want to witness alone.

Do you hear the theme of *fear* running throughout these responses? Fear that keeps us from doing evangelism is never from God (2 Tim. 1:7), so it must be from the Enemy. To counter that fear, we must design evangelism programs that address fears and counter the Enemy's schemes with truth and training (see Exhibit 4-4).

As you plan evangelism training, remember the rooftop of our model of a healthy church. Members of a healthy church live out their faith in their personal lives, in their church, in their home, and in their workplace. Healthy churches train discipled warriors to evangelize their families and coworkers. Faith lived out and proclaimed before nonbelievers is always a threat to the Enemy.

Of course, developing such a training program for evangelism will take significant effort and organization. But if the Enemy is scheming to hinder the work of the church, we set ourselves up for defeat if our efforts are haphazard and disorganized.

Exhibit 4-4 Evangelism Training Strategies

Fear . . .	Counterstrategy . . .
"I will make a mistake and be embarrassed."	Disciple believers. Help them to fall in love with God, for love willingly risks embarrassment. Send veteran evangelists to support and train rookies. Practice. Do role play. Share testimonies of overcoming embarrassment. Most people have been embarrassed when witnessing.
"I won't know what to say."	Train believers. Give them simple tools for remembering the gospel. Help believers to develop their own witnessing strategy, ensuring that the gospel is proclaimed. Develop prayer support teams. Remind believers that the Holy Spirit will help them know what to say.
"I won't know how to answer questions."	Give believers the permission not to know everything. The gospel is powerful, and the gospel we know. Train in apologetics. Give reasons for their faith while preparing them to counter lies that others believe. Examine possible excuses for rejecting the gospel. Arm the witnesses with truth.
"I am shy and do not want to witness alone."	Send out teams rather than individuals. Follow Jesus' model in Luke 10:1. Train mentors who invest in students who are learning. Enlist "formerly shy" individuals to share how God's grace and empowerment helped them overcome their fears.

Pray for one another.

The apostle Paul certainly knew the spiritual battles associated with evangelism. He was imprisoned for preaching the good news even as he wrote to the Ephesians to "put on the full armor of God" (Eph. 6:11). Paul, though, didn't run from the battle. Instead, he asked the Ephesians and the Colossians to *pray* for him:

> Pray on my behalf, that utterance may be given to me in the opening of my mouth, to make known with boldness the mystery of the gospel, for which I am an ambassador in chains; that in proclaiming it I may speak boldly, as I ought to speak. (Eph. 6:19–20)

> Devote yourselves to prayer, keeping alert in it with an attitude of thanksgiving; praying at the same time for us as well, that God will open up to us a door for the word, so that we may speak forth the mystery of Christ, for which I have also been imprisoned; that I may make it clear in the way I ought to speak. (Col. 4:2–4)

In the face of spiritual battles, Paul sought prayer support for boldness, clarity, and opportunities to share the gospel. He knew that Satan did not intend to give up his captives easily, and he understood that he could not reach unbelievers apart from the power of God. Paul so believed in the freeing power of the gospel that he did not want to miss a single opportunity to proclaim the truth with courage and clarity.

Paul, God's chosen apostle, preached before kings, suffered persecution, and paid a high price for his faith. He needed prayer support in order to be brave and clear when he evangelized. Do you suppose we might need prayer support, too? One Midwestern pastor asked his church to pray Ephesians 6:19–20 and Colossians 4:2–4 for him daily. He distributed the texts printed on a note card so that people are reminded to pray. Only God knows what will be the long-term results of these prayers, but I'm certain that the Enemy is now a little more alarmed by this pastor's leadership. Churches that pray this way for their leaders and for one another experience victory in evangelism. We will return to the topic of prayer in chapter 7.

Get involved.

Healthy churches "take advantage of every opportunity to [make an impact upon] the world for Christ," according to senior pastor Ted Haggard of New Life Church in Colorado Springs, Colorado.[6] Haggard's church is a model of a missions-minded congregation. Flags from every nation on earth hang in the auditorium. Church members take prayer journeys into regions that are closed to the gospel. The church has a goal of taking at least 100 high school students overseas each year to do missions. Intercessors around the world receive information through the World Prayer Center housed on New Life's property. New Life Church truly exists for those who have never heard about Jesus.

This church, however, is the exception to a general lack of commitment to the world. World population is projected to be 8.8 billion by 2020, of whom no more than 35 percent are expected to be Christians.[7] An estimated 95 percent of the unreached people live in the region 10 degrees to 40 degrees north of the equator, from West Africa to East Asia. This so-called "10/40 window" is home to about 3.6 billion people, whose religious lives are mostly taken up with Islam, Hinduism, Buddhism, and indigenous religions. More than 2000 distinct people groups, most located in the 10/40 window, do not have access to the gospel.

One of the most active and largest missions-minded evangelical denominations of the United States is the Southern Baptist Convention, which supports more than 5000 international missionaries. Yet even in this enormous missions program, hundreds of requests for missionaries remain unfilled. The world cries out for healthy churches who will invest themselves in reaching lost humanity, but there still are few laborers (see Luke 10:2). Leaders can do much to empower a church to be a "going and sending" force that is unafraid to engage the darkness.

Application

News of the Japanese surrender to the Allied powers, ending World War II, came to the United States after midnight on August 15, 1945. The "flash" announcement reverberated across radio waves: "Japanese radio has just been heard announcing the acceptance of surrender terms. The war is over!"[8]

Official notification would not come until the next evening, but Americans nevertheless celebrated in the streets, including that American sailor who became the symbol for "V. J. Day" when he was photographed kissing a young lady on a New York City street. Victory—especially victory over a ruthless enemy in a long war—is cause for celebration. If victory in earthly battles evokes such a response, how much more should we proclaim our victory over the Devil?

Our spiritual battles are real, but the Enemy has been disarmed by Jesus' death on the cross (Col. 2:15). His final destruction is assured (Rev. 12:7–9; 20:10). He battles against us, but we fight from a position of guaranteed victory. Ultimately, the Devil cannot win.

How can we not tell this good news to a lost and dying world? Keep outreach in front of the church. Use ideas such as the following to challenge your church to put on the armor, to see the world through God's eyes, and to step courageously into the darkness:

- Lead a study on the significant missionary passages of

the Old Testament, for example, the books of Isaiah and Jonah.

- Preach on Jesus' methods of evangelism.
- Survey to determine the obstacles people face in doing personal evangelism. Disciple with a strategy to overcome these particular obstacles.
- Conduct training seminars to prepare the church to reach out to people of other faiths. For example, a former Muslim can give solid advice for reaching out to Muslims.
- Train to counter the lies that evangelists hear from non-believers. Consider enlisting other churches in an area apologetics conference. Working together, you might be able to enlist the services of a leading thinker in this field.
- If you are a preacher, enlist a "sermon evaluation team" to evaluate your sermons for evangelistic effectiveness. Assess such issues as clarity and the use of religious jargon.
- Candidly evaluate your church's evangelistic track record. How many non-believers has your church reached in the last year? the last five years? How effectively is your congregation influencing your community through evangelism?
- Reach out to international students. Learn about their culture as you invite them to learn about your culture and faith.
- Plan a short-term mission to introduce your congregation to missions.
- Adopt an "unreached people group" on whom everyone will focus in prayer.
- Enlist a team of prayer warriors who will pray Ephesians 6:19–20 and Colossians 4:2–4 for your church leadership.
- Schedule missionaries to speak. Consider making a conference call during morning worship to missionaries in the field. Hear first hand from people on the front lines of battle.
- Plan evangelism training events, possibly focusing on

parents evangelizing their children and coworkers reaching coworkers.

- Provide baptismal announcements for new converts. Encourage them to use the announcements to invite family and friends to their baptism.
- Sponsor a "spiritual birthday party" for new believers to celebrate what God has done.

For further study

Beougher, Timothy, and Alvin Reid. *Evangelism for a Changing World.* Wheaton, Ill.: Harold Shaw, 1995.

Carson, D. A., ed. *Telling the Truth*. Grand Rapids: Zondervan, 2000.

Christenson, Evelyn. *Battling the Prince of Darkness: Rescuing Captives from Satan's Kingdom*. Wheaton, Ill.: Victor, 1990.

Coleman, Robert. *The Master's Way of Personal Evangelism*. Wheaton, Ill.: Crossway, 1997.

Eastman, Dick. *Love on Its Knees: Make a Difference by Praying for Others.* Tarrytown, N.Y.: Chosen, 1989.

Fay, William. *Share Jesus Without Fear*. Nashville: Broadman & Holman, 1999.

Kaiser, Walter C. Jr. *Mission in the Old Testament: Israel as a Light to the Nations*. Grand Rapids: Baker, 2000.

McCloskey, Mark. *Tell It Often, Tell It Well*. Eugene, Ore: Wipf & Stock, 1998.

Metzger, Will. *Tell the Truth*. Downers Grove, Ill.: InterVarsity, 1984.

Mittleberg, Mark. *Building a Contagious Church*. Grand Rapids: Zondervan, 2000.

Otis, George Jr., ed. *Strongholds of the 10/40 Window*. Seattle: Youth with a Mission, 1995.

Piper, John. *Let the Nations Be Glad! The Supremacy of God in Missions.* Grand Rapids: Baker, 1993.

Rainer, Thom S. *Surprising Insights from the Unchurched*. Grand Rapids: Zondervan, 2001.

Reid, Alvin. *Introduction to Evangelism*. Nashville: Broadman & Holman, 1998.
Sjogren, Steve. *Conspiracy of Kindness*. Ann Arbor, Mich.: Vine, 1993.
Terry, John Mark. *Church Evangelism*. Nashville: Broadman & Holman, 1997.
——, et al., eds. *Missiology*. Nashville: Broadman & Holman, 1998.

Notes

1. Robert Garrett, "The Gospel and Acts: Jesus the Missionary and His Missionary Followers," in *Missiology* (Nashville: Broadman & Holman, 1998), 63.
2. Avery Willis, "The Unfinished Task," in *Missiology*, eds. John Mark Terry, Ebbie Smith, and Justice Anderson (Nashville: Broadman & Holman, 1998), 668.
3. Randy Alcorn, *Lord Foulgrin's Letters* (Sisters, Ore.: Multnomah, 2000), 192, 193. Emphasis added.
4. See Timothy Beougher, *Overcoming Walls to Witnessing* (Minneapolis: Billy Graham Evangelistic Association, 1993).
5. *On Mission*, September–October 1998: 26.
6. Ted Haggard, *The Life Giving Church* (Ventura: Regal, 2001), 160.
7. Jerry Rankin, "The Present Situation in Missions," in *Missiology* (Nashville: Broadman & Holman, 1998), 32–33.
8. Joe Garner, *We Interrupt This Broadcast* (Naperville, Ill.: Sourcebooks, 1998), 26–28.

CHAPTER 5

Discipled Warriors Equipping Believers

Matthew 28:18–20; Acts 2:42

During a conference for Christian singles on a United States Air Force base in Asia, one of the pilots took me to the flight line and allowed me to sit in the cockpit of a jet fighter. For one with a special interest in military aircraft, it was an exciting moment. This instrument of war could travel faster than the speed of sound and drop ordnance precisely from high altitudes.

Imagining what it would be like to fly one of these machines into battle was one thing. Had I actually been asked to do it, I would have had a significant problem. I was at the controls of the plane, but I had no idea how to fly it. The equipment was there, but I had not been equipped. As a pilot, I would have been more dangerous to the support crew at the airbase than to an enemy.

No one would think of putting an untrained civilian at the controls of a state-of-the-art warplane, but we think nothing of sending troops into spiritual warfare without a proper understanding of God's arsenal to live victoriously. We are more of a threat to the church than to the Enemy. Healthy churches that win spiritual battles take the time to equip believers through teaching and mentoring. Discipled warriors know how to walk obediently and how to stand firmly against the Enemy.

Our Calling to Equip Believers

Spiritual warfare, as emphasized in the book of Ephesians, is central to our model of a healthy church that overcomes the Enemy. Chapters 1–3 lay the theological foundation, and chapters 4–6 apply this theology to Christian living. That makes 4:1 the fulcrum and moves the reader into a discussion about "equipping the saints." Follow Paul's argument:

4:1	We must walk worthy of all that God has done for us (as described in Ephesians 1–3).
4:2	Such a walk exhibits humility, gentleness, patience, and tolerance or forbearance.
4:3–6	This attitude toward others preserves unity, for there is one body, one Spirit, one Lord, one faith, one baptism, and one God and Father.
4:7	Unity does not mean a lack of diversity. On the contrary, God in Christ has enabled the body by providing significant individual gifts for the work (vv. 8–10).
4:11–12	God gives leaders to equip all of the saints to do the work of the church. As believers obey their callings, the body is built.
4:13	When believers take their individual places, unity and spiritual maturity result. The church moves toward the goal of exhibiting the attributes of Christ.
4:14	Mature, equipped believers will not be tossed about by false teaching.
4:15	Equipping demands living and speaking the truth in love so that growing members continue to mature.
4:16	The healthy church is characterized by individual members—each equipped and maturing—serving together. These members walk in a manner worthy of their calling, and the church is united, even in its diversity.

What, then, is equipping? The word translated "equip" in Ephesians 4:12 also was used for setting a broken bone or mending a torn net. Philosophers used the term to speak of guiding people to fulfill their purpose. Paul employed the word to describe the work of church leaders who "engage in the practical preparation or training of the saints" so church members might obey their calling.[1]

Of the word Paul used, one New Testament scholar said, "The notion of equipping or preparing, in the sense of making someone adequate or sufficient for something, best suits the context. However, it does require an object: people are prepared for some purpose."[2] Thus, a primary goal of equipping is to prepare believers to *do something in the ministry of the church.*

Although *equipping* refers to broader preparation than simply teaching and modeling practical skills, it does assume action on the part of the equipped. In an equipping church, . . .

- members are taught and expected to witness.
- teachers are trained to teach, and then they are placed in teaching roles.
- group leaders receive training and are rotated into group leadership.
- choir members are challenged to learn and grow musically, even as they sing God's praises.
- worshipers learn about true worship.
- members are taught to pray and challenged to do so.
- deacons are trained in caring skills and then held accountable to do ministry.
- all members of the body are expected to serve in the capacity for which they are trained.
- leaders teach and train the members, laying a theological foundation and guiding them to live out their faith through the ministries of the church.

Maybe this description helps you to understand why I differentiate between "disciplemaking" and "equipping." Disciplemaking is the overall process of guiding believers to be followers of Jesus. Included in that process is everything from building a theological foundation to carrying the gospel to the ends of the earth.

Equipping, on the other hand, is one essential component of disciplemaking. An equipping church strives to produce discipled warriors trained to faithfully carry out the ministry of the church.

Strategies of the Enemy

Church A is a medium-sized church in the Midwest. They have baptized an average of twenty-five new converts a year for several years. At the same time, there is no intentional strategy to train and equip these believers. They reach people for Christ, but their attendance seldom changes. Volunteers come and go, and pastors typically stay two or three years. Conflict is common.

Church B is a vibrant congregation in Colorado. This church requires prospective members to attend an orientation class, guides members to understand their spiritual gifts, and expects them to get involved in ministry. Their growth is consistent and steady. Equipping events occur year round.

In Church A, few members (including most of the current leaders) have been really trained to do the work of the church. A majority of the members in Church B have been trained, and they are serving according to their giftedness and training. How do you think the Enemy might attack these two churches?

Attacks on the unequipped body

In Church A, Satan will find vulnerable targets among members who have not been equipped to carry out the ministry of the church but have been placed in leadership by default.

Unequipped leaders are susceptible to pride. We would assume that a new convert is unequipped for a leadership position because he might "become conceited and fall into the condemnation incurred by the devil" (1 Tim. 3:6). Yet, even some long-term believers reflect the spiritual depth of a new convert. They are often leaders but lack the training needed to lead effectively. In truth, they are neither disciples nor warriors.

Leaders who are not spiritually and practically equipped for leadership may become arrogant and begin to flaunt their authority. In the end, they lose their witness inside and outside of the church, snared by the same arrogance that caused the devil to fall (1 Tim. 3:6–7). Satan, who himself was entrapped by pride, now sets the same trap for unequipped leaders.

Peter had experienced a powerful conversion from drug and alcohol addiction. Within a few weeks after his conversion, he was telling his story in churches. His own church asked him to teach a class of young men. Leaders reasoned that Peter could help these youths avoid his own mistakes. But they did not help Peter to grow or prepare him for his leadership responsibility. He was not guided in prayer and Bible study, nor given the opportunity to learn discernment.

Six months later, Peter was arrested as he bought drugs on the street. He had returned to using drugs and pornography within two months of his conversion, but he had no accountability structure nor anyone to whom he could go for help. His pride at overcoming his addictions had set him up for failure, compounded by his pride at being given spiritual leadership without spiritual discipleship. Obviously, he failed in his choices, but those who were using him because he had a dramatic testimony had much for which to answer. They showed a lack of concern for this new believer and unwittingly shoved him toward the Devil's trap.

Unequipped members are targets for attacks of discouragement. Have you ever tried to serve God, only to be more defeated than ever? Julie suffered that experience as a young Sunday school teacher. She was bright, excited, and bubbling with joy when her church leaders nominated her to teach a first grade children's class. The education director gave her a teacher's book, pointed her to the room, and thanked her for her willingness to serve. At no point did he offer her training for this important ministry.

On her first Sunday, Julie was not prepared for fifteen rambunctious six-year-olds. Nobody had taken the time to explain to her the material in the teacher's manual. No one had taught her how to teach at the level of first graders. Worse yet, she had been given no principles for disciplining children without breaking their spirit. She left class that first Sunday, defeated and discouraged.

Surprisingly, her education director only patted her on the shoulder and said, "Hang in there. It'll get better." But, nothing improved before Julie resigned her class six months later. Today, she wonders if God will ever use her in the church.

Do you see what happened? Julie was placed in a position for which she was not equipped, making her vulnerable to the Enemy's messages. "You're just not good enough to teach." "They're not listening to you, anyway. You're wasting your time." "You're just a babysitter." "If you were any kind of a Christian, you'd be doing a better job." "Just give up"—and she did. Churches who do not equip their members for service set them up for attacks of discouragement from the Enemy.

Not surprisingly, churches that do not disciple and prepare members tend to foster inactivity. By choosing not to equip and hold people accountable, the leaders of Church A give them permission to fill spaces at worship and then slip out untapped. Members join but do not get involved. They sit in the pew, waiting for their needs to be met. No one expects much from them, and no one gets much from them.

Some of these unchallenged members eventually drift out and do not return. Others assume that casual Christianity is acceptable, and their witness is poor. For many people, sin "crouches at the door" because they are not focused on becoming men and women of God (see Gen. 4:7). Complacency leads to an unguarded heart—and the Enemy aims his arrows at unguarded hearts.

Why do most churches have many more members than they do active attenders? In many cases, members on the rolls are not true believers. At the same time, though, other genuine believers joined churches that expected nothing from them. Their churches didn't challenge them to serve, nor did they equip them for service. The Enemy aimed his arrows at these members and found them to be vulnerable targets. Now, they're not even attending church where at least they may hear the Word that can set them free.

Attacks on the equipped body

Church B obviously is healthier and would seem to be immune to Satan's attacks. That's not the case. Attacks here are more subtle, but they are no less potent. The difference is that the equipping church is more likely to be prepared for the battle.

Equippers themselves are susceptible to attack. God gives us church leaders to equip us, so it stands to reason that the Enemy would focus on them. When leaders fall, one consequence is that the primary equippers in the church lose their influence. Why should I accept spiritual challenges from someone who has not lived up to God's expectations? Satan has other reasons for attacking leaders, but hindering the equipping process is a primary one.

The master preacher Charles Spurgeon described this reality to his ministry students:

> Recollect, as ministers, that your whole life, your whole pastoral life especially, will be affected by the vigour of your piety. . . . When your soul becomes lean, your hearers, without knowing how or why, will find that your prayers in public have little savour for them; they will feel your barrenness, perhaps, before you perceive it

> yourself. . . . In your daily communion with your people, they will not be slow to mark the all-pervading decline of your graces. . . . Moreover, as the result of your own decline, everyone of your hearers will suffer more or less; the vigorous amongst them will overcome the depressing tendency, but the weaker sort will be seriously damaged. . . . The great enemy of souls takes care to leave no stone unturned for the preacher's ruin [for] he knows what a rout he can make among the rest, if the leaders fall before their eyes.[3]

Spiritual leaders have to be aware of this temptation to "leanness." Two basic principles help leaders guard against Satan's attacks.

First, leaders are vulnerable to the Enemy when they think themselves strong enough to conquer the Enemy.

Most of those who are trained for leadership can accomplish quite a bit by virtue of their organizational and oratorical skills. That self-confidence makes leaders vulnerable to the temptation of working in their own strength.

Think about it this way. When you ask others to pray for you, you usually seek prayers about areas of weakness. We are aware of our needs for help in such areas. We are less inclined to ask for prayers in the areas of our strengths. We assume that we *don't* need help there, so our guard is down. Our unguarded strength becomes a reason for pride. Strength leads to pride, which leads to a fall (Prov. 16:18).

Second, leaders who work alone are asking for the Enemy's attacks. We are most susceptible when we are alone, and ministers can spend much time working without a colaborer—in the office, making hospital visits, counseling, going to meetings across town or the nation. All the while, the Enemy waits to snare us with temptations.

Like the prodigal son, we often find it easiest to live riotously when we are farthest from accountability (Luke 15:11–

13). Remember, the Enemy lurks in darkness—where no one is watching. The Enemy loves to lead us into hidden sin and then to turn on a blazing light so that everyone knows we have failed.

The Enemy also leads "equipped" believers to misuse their spiritual gifts. Spiritual gift inventories became a hot item in the 1980s and 1990s. Church leaders across the nation challenged members to take a test to "discover" their spiritual gifts. Some results of this attention on gifts were positive. Churches began to take seriously God's gifts that enable the body of Christ to function (1 Cor. 12:1–30). A corresponding emphasis on equipping the laity strengthened the church.

Negatively, however, some churches assumed that members who completed a gifts inventory were automatically "equipped" to use their gifts. For instance, members with the gift of teaching were enlisted to teach with little or no training. People with the gift of administration were given significant administrative roles for which they were not prepared.

In addition, others whose gift inventory indicated the gift of "prophecy" began announcing "authoritative" messages from God. Like the Corinthians of centuries before (1 Corinthians 12–14), some claimed that their gifts were more significant than others. The result was often chaos and division—marks of the Enemy's hand rather than God's.

Equipping is much more than simply helping members determine their spiritual gifts. The Enemy wants the church to become self-focused on their gifts, but a healthy church guides members to use their gifts in ways that are edifying to the church (Eph. 4:12). Healthy churches use their gifts to strengthen and build up one another.

The Enemy infiltrates "equipping" churches through bad doctrine. In a 1990s study, George Barna discovered that approximately one million people a year receive some type of evangelism training. As many as sixty million people shared their faith with someone during the year before the study, and 47 percent of those had received some training.[4]

Assuming that Barna's findings are accurate, some churches in America *are* equipping their members for evangelism. The continued success of such programs as *Evangelism Explosion, How to Become a Contagious Christian*, and the *F.A.I.T.H.* Sunday school evangelism strategy also indicates that equipping is taking place.

But there is a dark side to this trend, however. Barna raises the concern that, among those who said they were sharing their faith,

- one-fourth did not believe the Bible is accurate in all that it teaches;
- one-third believed that people who are good enough will earn a place in heaven;
- two-fifths believed that all faiths teach similar lessons about life, so a person's beliefs ultimately do not matter; and
- one-fourth said that Jesus made mistakes.

Barna concluded that one-third of those who shared their faith probably weren't true believers themselves.[5] Apparently, some churches were equipping members to do something—evangelism—without first teaching the gospel they needed to share.

Notice the subtle deception behind this strategy. The church is doing the right action but teaching the wrong doctrine. Ironically, church members are doing evangelism, but their very theology will weaken their commitment to evangelism in the long run. Evangelism equipping, I suspect, will eventually end in churches that do not believe that all non-Christians must experience a personal relationship with Jesus.

Here, the necessity of a strong theological foundation is again apparent. Healthy churches that equip effectively focus on the Word of God, training believers so that they are not "tossed here and there by waves and carried about by every wind of doctrine" (Eph. 4:14).

The Healthy Church Stands Armed

Most churches are a combination of the nonequipping Church A and the equipping Church B. Their pastoral leaders and some members (albeit only a few) have been trained. The rest are not equipped to do ministry. Consider implementing the following recommendations to grow a healthy congregation that stands armed against the Enemy.

Enlist a prayer team to pray for leaders/equippers.

Pastors/teachers are to be equippers, and Satan does not want the church to be equipped. Thus, he targets the equippers so that their lives lack credibility–and so that no one will listen as they challenge people to be faithful. To help pastoral leaders guard against the Enemy's attacks, enlist prayer teams that pray specifically, intentionally, and faithfully for them. The effective prayer of righteous believers will make a difference in the lives of those called to equip them (James 5:16).

A young married man became sexually involved with a woman. Members of the church where he was a lay leader were shocked. What caught my attention as I read an account of this tragedy, though, was the unique reaction of one church member. She wondered if the man would have fallen into sin if the other church members had not taken his strength for granted. What might have happened differently, she asked, if they had been praying for him *before* they heard about his trouble? Healthy churches *protect* their leaders through prayer.

Prayer teams should pray specifically that their leaders . . .

- have a spirit of humility (Col. 3:12; 1 Peter 5:5).
- maintain their time with God (2 Tim. 2:15).
- lead in their families (Eph. 5:25; 6:4).

- have victory over sin (1 Cor. 10:13).
- be faithful evangelists (Eph. 6:19–20).
- will equip others effectively (Eph. 4:11–12).

Hold members accountable for their privileges *and* responsibilities.

Chapter 2 discussed the privilege and responsibility of church membership. The Enemy focuses our attention on the *privileges* rather than on the *responsibilities* as a way of shifting our focus toward self. People who are obsessed with what the church should do for them are thinking little about their service to the Lord. On the other hand, members of a healthy body know that each member has a role to play. They understand that even a single uncommitted member weakens the entire body (1 Cor. 12:14–26).

One way to hold believers accountable for their responsibilities is to implement a membership covenant. A few denominations mandate a standard covenant to be used throughout their churches. Our research at the Billy Graham School has shown that churches that raise the standards of membership (often through the use of a covenant) ultimately produce members who are more committed, better equipped, and more outward focused.[6] Exhibit 5-1 is a sample covenant that expresses both the privileges and responsibilities of church membership. Chapter 9 offers other suggestions for instilling high expectations.

Recognize, however, that churches that hold their members accountable must take responsibility to equip the members. High expectations accompanied by systematic equipping result in a congregation that honors God and threatens the Enemy.

Exhibit 5-1 Model Membership Covenant

Having received Jesus Christ as my Lord and Savior, I believe that the Holy Spirit is directing me to join the family of Christian believers at ______________________________ Church.

In joining this community of the body of Christ, I commit myself before God and the other members to do the following:

1. I will faithfully support the work of the church through my regular attendance and giving.

   Bring the whole tithe into the storehouse (Mal. 3:10)

   For God loves a cheerful giver. (2 Cor. 9:7b)

   And let us consider how to stimulate one another to love and good deeds, not forsaking our own assembling together, as is the habit of some, but encouraging one another. (Heb. 10:24–25)

2. I will support the witness of the church by . . .

   - Studying and following God's Word.

     Your word I have treasured in my heart, That I may not sin against You. (Ps. 119:11)

     All Scripture is inspired by God and profitable for teaching, for reproof, for correction, for training in righteousness; so that the man of God may be adequate, equipped for every good work. (2 Tim. 3:16–17)

   - Praying consistently for our leaders and members.

     Pray for us, for we are sure that we have a good conscience, desiring to conduct ourselves honorably in all things. (Heb. 13:18)

     Pray for one another. (James 5:16b)

Exhibit 5-1 continued

- Living my life in a God-honoring way.

Therefore I, the prisoner of the Lord, implore you to walk in a manner worthy of the calling with which you have been called. (Eph. 4:1)

Only conduct yourselves in a manner worthy of the gospel of Christ, so that whether I come and see you or remain absent, I will hear of you that you are standing firm in one spirit, with one mind striving together for the faith of the gospel. (Phil. 1:27)

3. I will serve by using my spiritual gifts in ministry.

But to each one is given the manifestation of the Spirit for the common good. . . . But one and the same Spirit works all these things, distributing to each one individually just as He wills. (1 Cor. 12:7, 11)

As each one has received a special gift, employ it in serving one another as good stewards of the manifold grace of God. (1 Peter 4:10)

4. I will seek and take advantage of opportunities to tell others about the good news of Jesus—including supporting and praying for missionaries around the world.

And pray on my behalf, that utterance may be given to me in the opening of my mouth, to make known with boldness the mystery of the gospel, for which I am an ambassador in chains; that in proclaiming it I may speak boldly, as I ought to speak. (Eph. 6:19–20)

Go therefore and make disciples of all the nations, baptizing them in the name of the Father and the Son and the Holy Spirit, teaching them to observe all that I commanded you; and lo, I am with you always, even to the end of the age. (Matt. 28:19–20)

____________________________ ____________

Member's signature Date

____________________________ ____________

Pastor's signature Date

Help members discern how God has prepared them for service.

Although Christians sometimes misuse the concept of spiritual gifts, that does not mean spiritual gifts can be ignored. God has given our members spiritual gifts for the work of the church (1 Cor. 12:7; 1 Peter 4:10), and we must help them to recognize and use their gifts. At the same time, we should guide our members to examine all of the possibilities of ways that God has prepared them to serve.

Authors Rick Warren and Wayne Cordeiro help us here.[7] They challenge people to examine all of their lives, including their spiritual gifts. Exhibit 5-2 (p. 120) compares Warren's SHAPE and Cordeiro's DESIGN approaches.

From a spiritual warfare perspective, I am especially grateful for the *E* designation in the models of both Warren and Cordeiro. Christians are shaped by life experiences—not all of them positive. Sometimes we retain bitterness and anger from the past, but negative events can also help shape us in a positive way. They prepare us to minister to others who face similar experiences.

For example, Satan attacked Job with a vengeance (see Job 1–2) with God's permission. If anyone had a right to be bitter toward God, it was Job. But Job trusted God, even as he questioned and struggled. Today, we turn to Job for insight when we face unexplained struggles. Whatever Job's spiritual gifts, his experiences minister to us.

God's hand was on Job's life, even when Satan launched violent assaults against him and his family. When we realize that God sovereignly uses even our negative experiences, we are armed to overcome the Enemy.

Train members to do what God has called them to do.

As we've seen, sometimes our Enemy finds the church vulnerable simply because he is a better strategist. He launches

Exhibit 5-2 God Prepares for Service

The Question: How has God created, molded, and changed me so that I am who I am—ready to be further equipped for service?

Rick Warren's SHAPE concept	**Wayne Cordeiro's DESIGN concept**
Spiritual gifts—What gifts have I received?	**D**esire—What is my passion?
Heart—What are my passions?	**E**xperience—What life experiences have helped to make me who I am?
Abilities—What can I do?	**S**piritual gifts—What gifts have I received?
Personality—What kind of personality do I have?	**I**ndividual style—What is my personality temperament?
Experiences—What life experiences have shaped me?	**G**rowth phase—Where am I in my personal spiritual journey?
	Natural abilities—What *can* I do?

Comparison chart adapted from:
Rick Warren, *The Purpose Driven Church* (Grand Rapids: Zondervan, 1995), 369–70.
Wayne Cordeiro, *Doing Church as a Team* (Ventura, Calif.: Regal, 2001), 67–72.

aggressive schemes while we are still trying to figure out what programs to use, what order of worship to follow, and how many chairs we need for the fellowship meeting. Such concerns are important, but we can resolve many of them quickly and efficiently through an intentional plan that is developed around a clear vision and a thoughtful statement of purpose.

This is especially evident with regard to equipping. Julie, the teacher thrown to the six-year-olds, was enlisted in a church that lacked a plan for training. Had her church intentionally given her training under a veteran, plus plenty of educational resources for the age group and a helper or two, she could have had victory over Satan's attack. That reality hit home in her church, but by then it was too late to help Julie.

Cordeiro's church, New Hope Christian Fellowship in Honolulu, expects members to be involved in ministry. The title of one of Cordeiro's books, *Doing Church as a Team*, is a good summary of his philosophy. To enlist and train, he encourages *shadowing*, or "simply following someone around who has been serving in an area of interest to you."[8] Potential workers watch ministry getting done, do ministry under the supervision of an equipper, and learn how to minister on their own. Once they are in ministry positions, they are expected to equip others to serve alongside them.

This church has a strategic plan to equip members that has helped them grow from a handful of members in 1995 to more than eight thousand members today. New Hope is threatening the Enemy in Honolulu.

How might ministry improve if we equip members for the work of the church? Think about the number of ministry/service positions in your church, all of which will be more effective if people in those positions have been properly equipped: Sunday school teachers, missions organization leaders, trustees, deacons, elders, ushers, greeters, money counters, choir members, instrumentalists, evangelists, mentors, music directors, youth leaders, preschool and children's leaders, shepherds, parking lot attendants, disciplers, sound technicians, committee members, janitors, pastoral caregivers, outreach leaders, small group leaders. . . . *Every* member of the church should be equipped.

A healthy church that wins spiritual warfare has a strategy in place to teach members how to fulfill their callings.

Develop a mentoring program.

One of the best strategies for equipping believers is mentoring, *a God-given relationship in which one growing Christian encourages and equips another believer to reach his or her potential as a disciple of Christ.*[9] Mentoring is clearly evident in Scripture, so our model of a healthy church speaks of "equipping believers through teaching *and mentoring.*"

From Moses and Joshua, to Jesus and the disciples, to Paul and Timothy, mentoring was a foundational strategy of discipling. Jesus—the model Mentor—called His disciples to "be with Him" (Mark 3:14; Acts 1:21–22), and their being with Him caught the attention of the pagan world (Acts 4:13). The world marked the difference in people who had been with Jesus.

Men and women preparing for ministry at my seminary commonly request a mentor. I regret that I don't have time to meet all of these requests. I regret even more that these young ministers are often looking for a mentor because no one in their church took time to mentor them. This desire for mentoring relationships isn't limited to seminary students, however. Barna's research indicates that 77 percent of church members think that a discipleship/mentoring relationship would be "very valuable."[10]

Consider how an effective mentoring program in a local church might counter the Enemy's strategies:

- Leaders never work alone, so they are less vulnerable. They are always equipping someone.
- New believers have someone to walk alongside them and support them when they face attacks from the Enemy.
- Accountability and expectations for Christian living are built into the mentoring program.
- Believers are intentionally supporting each other through prayer.
- Mentors equip, and the one who is equipped equips an-

other. No one is given permission to sit in the church without serving.

- Mentoring models Jesus' method of equipping–and we are always more effective when we follow Jesus' example. Discipled warriors are mentored warriors.

Application

In January 1991, a coalition army led by the United States entered Kuwait to dislodge Iraqi troops that had invaded that country. Many of these warriors were not yet twenty years old, yet weapons of incredibly destructive power were put into their hands. I remember being alarmed that these warriors were so young. The conflict was short-lived, though, partly because these young military personnel were incredibly well prepared. Yes, they were controlling weapons of destruction, but they had been trained to do so. As a result, they overcame the enemy.

May God help His church to equip believers with that same intentionality and intensity. The following ideas will help you lead your church to equip discipled warriors through teaching and mentoring.

- Lead a study on Ephesians 4, focusing on the equipping texts.
- Preach a sermon series on Jesus' strategy for equipping the disciples. Show how God invests in the lives of others.
- Design a strategic plan to train each group of leaders in your church. Equip everyone from the parking lot attendants to the staff members. This work will take some time and energy, but faithfulness to Ephesians 4:11–12 demands that sacrifice.
- Conduct training seminars specifically designed to train teachers. Hold the teachers accountable, just as God does (James 3:1).
- Begin to lay the groundwork for adopting a church covenant. Work to get the support of your key church leaders.

- Enlist prayer teams to pray for specific groups of workers. For example, enlist (and train) a prayer team who will pray for the teachers, a team who will pray for the choir, a team who will pray for the ushers, etc. Assume that every worker needs prayer support.
- Survey your congregation to discover how many would be willing to be more active in service if the church provided training and support. In one church 60 percent of the adults not involved in ministry were simply waiting to be asked and trained.
- Schedule a training time to lead your church through the SHAPE or DESIGN process. Be prepared to follow up on church members who complete the analysis. Equip them to do ministry that fits their profiles.
- Be a mentor to one or two believers. Set an example for other church members.
- Enlist someone who is trained in family ministry to equip parents to raise their children under God's direction. Consider other opportunities to equip family members to serve one another, for example the parents of teenagers or adult children who care for aging parents.
- Ask a strong Christian layperson to equip members to be witnesses in their workplace.
- Study the use of covenants or membership standards in the history of your denomination or church.
- Lead a Bible study on mentors of the Bible, such as Moses, Jesus, and Paul.
- Send a team to study another church that is doing equipping well. Learn from other local bodies of Christ.

For further study

Anderson, Lynn. *They Smell Like Sheep*. West Monroe, La.: Howard, 1997.

Arn, Win, and Charles Arn. *The Master's Plan for Making Disciples.* Grand Rapids: Baker, 1998.

Biehl, Bobb. *Mentoring: Confidence in Finding a Mentor and Becoming One.* Nashville: Broadman & Holman, 1996.

Bunyan, John. *The Pilgrim's Progress.* Rev. by L. Edward Hazelbaker. North Brunswick, N.J.: Bridge-Logos, 1998.

Coleman, Robert. *The Master Plan of Evangelism.* Grand Rapids: Baker, 1993.

Coleman, Robert, et al., eds. *Disciplemaking.* Wheaton, Ill.: Billy Graham Center, 1994.

Elmore, Tim. *Mentoring: How to Invest Your Life in Others.* Atlanta: Equip, 1998.

Fryling, Alice. *Disciplemaker's Handbook.* Downers Grove, Ill.: InterVarsity, 1989.

Gangel, Kenneth O. *Unwrap Your Spiritual Gifts.* Wheaton, Ill.: Victor, 1994.

Hemphill, Ken. *Mirror, Mirror on the Wall: Discovering Your True Self Through Spiritual Gifts.* Nashville: Lifeway, 1992.

Hull, Bill. *The Disciplemaking Pastor.* Old Tappan, N.J.: Revell, 1988.

Longenecker, Richard, ed. *Patterns of Discipleship in the New Testament.* Grand Rapids: Eerdmans, 1996.

McClung, Floyd. *Basic Discipleship.* Downers Grove, Ill.: InterVarsity, 1990.

Malphurs, Aubrey. *Strategy 2000: Churches Making Disciples for the New Millennium.* Grand Rapids: Kregel, 1996.

Maxwell, John. *Developing the Leaders Around You.* Nashville: Thomas Nelson, 1995.

Notes

1. Margaret Y. MacDonald, *Colossians and Ephesians*, Sacra Pagina (Collegeville, Minn.: Liturgical, 2000), 292.
2. Peter T. O'Brien, *The Letter to the Ephesians*, The Pillar New Testament Commentary (Grand Rapids: Eerdmans, 1999), 303.

3. Charles Spurgeon, *Lectures to My Students* (repr. ed., Grand Rapids: Zondervan, 1954), 15–16.
4. George Barna, Evangelism That Works (Ventura, Calif.: Regal, 1995), 71–73.
5. Ibid., 142.
6. See Thom S. Rainer, *High Expectations* (Nashville: Broadman & Holman, 1998).
7. See Rick Warren, *The Purpose Driven Church* (Grand Rapids: Zondervan, 1995), 369–70; and Wayne Cordeiro, *Doing Church as a Team* (Ventura, Calif.: Regal, 2001), 67–72.
8. Cordeiro, *Doing Church*, 114.
9. This definition includes several important elements. First, mentoring takes place within a *God-given* relationship. Second, the mentor is himself growing in his/her Christian walk. Third, mentoring includes both encouragement (giving confidence through support) and equipping (providing tools and training for tasks). Fourth, the mentor challenges the mentee to strive for God's best. See my work, *Making Disciples Through Mentoring* (Lynchburg, Va.: Church Growth Institute, 2002).
10. George Barna, *Growing True Disciples* (Ventura, Calif.: Issachar Resources, 2000), 46.

CHAPTER 6

Discipled Warriors Edifying Others

Matthew 22:39; Acts 2:44–45

First Baptist Church of Leesburg, Florida, is a dynamic congregation known for investing millions of dollars and thousands of hours of labor in its "ministry village." In this "village" are more than seventy different projects, including shelters for the homeless; a pregnancy care center; counseling and support groups; and a Christian school, day care, and after-school program.[1]

Charlotte Rubush was a drug addict just released from jail when she was part of the Women's Care Center. She eventually became a believer and now teaches one of the weekly Bible studies at the Care Center. Charlotte was in the Enemy's grip when this local church reached out to her. Christ set her free, and she is quick to proclaim that she is "drug free, debt free, and spiritually free."[2] Now, she serves others as a discipled warrior in a healthy church.

Our Calling to Edify in Ministry and Service

In our spiritual war, we also occasionally need someone to encourage and build us up. The healthy church offers this kind of ministry–a ministry that edifies and challenges others to press on in the battle.

Love your neighbor.

Jesus responded to questions from the religious leaders of His day with answers that were at times not always direct but always right. When leaders demanded to know where He got authority to drive moneychangers from the temple, He asked them about the authority of John the Baptist (Matt. 21:23–27). When they quizzed Him about paying taxes, He used a coin as an object lesson (22:15–22). When they asked about marriage in heaven, He pointed out their unbelief and reminded them that God is the God of the living (vv. 23–33).

At other times, Jesus responded with undeniable clarity, as when a lawyer asked Him which of the commandments is the greatest. "You shall love the Lord your God with all your heart, and with all your soul, and with all your mind. This is the great and foremost commandment," Jesus answered (Matt. 22:37–38). But then Jesus' response went beyond the question to add a second commandment: "The second is like it, 'You shall love your neighbor as yourself.' On these two commandments depend the whole Law and the Prophets" (vv. 39–40).

In answering one question with two responses, Jesus taught that these commandments are inseparable. Indeed, all other commandments are summarized in these two. If we say that we love God but hate others, we are only liars (1 John 4:20). If we say that we love others but do not truly love God, our love for others is only altruism. Genuine love for God is expressed in genuine love toward others.

The word translated "love" in Matthew 22:39 is *agapē*, a word that speaks of voluntary, giving love. *Agapē* love is an action love expressed in compassion and benevolence toward others, even when we don't "feel like it." This kind of love is evident in believers who feed the hungry and thirsty, welcome the stranger, clothe the needy, visit the sick, and reach out to the prisoner (25:31–46). This love was also apparent in the early church, as they shared all they had with all who were in need (Acts 2:44–45).

Southeast Christian Church in Louisville, Kentucky, models this kind of servant love. One of the largest churches in the country, Southeast sponsors an annual "Great Day of Service," during which members help at jobs throughout the community. Pastor Bob Russell says that this day provides opportunities to minister to neighbors *and* to love one another: "We painted rooms, cleaned windows, stuffed envelopes, planted flowers, and served in whatever capacity was needed. Not only do such service projects help to meet the needs of the community and provide great opportunities for witness, they're also great times of fellowship. You feel a kinship with someone who stood beside you painting all day, who planted flowers with you, or who helped you clean windows."[3]

Discipled warriors love God, love one another, and love the unreached. They also *do something* with their faith, including ministering to those who have little to offer in return. Healthy churches produce that kind of warrior.

Serve one another.

If we are to love one another with a love expressed in action, we should expect the Bible to offer some detail about *how* to love others. A sampling of "one another" passages in the New Testament displays snapshots of how we are to love:

- "Be devoted to one another in brotherly love; give preference to one another in honor" (Rom. 12:10).
- "Be of the same mind toward one another; do not be haughty in mind, but associate with the lowly" (Rom. 12:16).
- "Accept one another, just as Christ also accepted us to the glory of God" (Rom. 15:7).
- "Through love serve one another" (Gal. 5:13).
- "Bear one another's burdens, and thereby fulfill the law of Christ" (Gal. 6:2).

- "Walk . . . with patience, showing tolerance for one another in love" (Eph. 4:1–2).
- "Be kind to one another, tender-hearted, forgiving each other, just as God in Christ also has forgiven you" (Eph. 4:32).
- "Put on a heart of compassion . . . bearing with one another, and forgiving each other" (Col. 3:12–13).
- "Let the word of Christ richly dwell within you, with all wisdom teaching and admonishing one another with psalms and hymns and spiritual songs, singing with thankfulness in your hearts to God" (Col. 3:16).
- "Therefore encourage one another and build up one another" (1 Thess. 5:11).
- "Let us consider how to stimulate one another to love and good deeds" (Heb. 10:24).
- "Therefore, confess your sins to one another, and pray for one another so that you may be healed" (James 5:16).
- "Fervently love one another from the heart" (1 Peter 1:22b).

Scripture calls us to minister to and serve others—precisely the opposite of what the Enemy wants us to do. His goal is to get us to focus on ourselves and to ignore others.

At the same time, focusing on others is one way to *counter* many of the Enemy's attacks. Believers who serve others and give them preference counter the temptation of pride. Those who bear one another's burdens provide support when the battles become intense. Accepting and forgiving others breaks the strongholds of prejudice and bitterness. Likewise, confessing sins to those who provide encouragement and prayer weakens the Enemy's hold.

At First Baptist Church of Leesburg, Florida, more than fourteen hundred members fill volunteer positions in the church's ministries. To keep these volunteers equipped and encouraged, the church provides a holistic support system. They offer programs for physical fitness as well as spiritual growth. The church provides support and training for members who are struggling financially. Life-skills training in such areas as parenting is an essential component of the church's strategy for growth.

Charles Roesel knows the connection between ministering to members and growing a ministering church: "If we don't keep our own family healthy, . . . it will not be able to minister to others. . . . We have found that ministering to, loving, and encouraging the church family develop effective ministers and witnesses."[4]

Church members who serve one another are best prepared to minister to others. Healthy churches produce "servant troops" who support each other, even as they reach beyond the church.

Build others through ministry.

Remember that the purpose of the church covered in this chapter is to edify others through ministry and service. I have specific reasons for using the term *edify* (besides the fact that another word beginning with "e" best fits my model).

First, Paul told the Ephesians to equip the saints "for the work of service, to the building up of the body of Christ" (Eph. 4:12). As we noted in the last chapter, equipping assumes that believers will do ministry. Each member fulfills his or her calling in the church, and the entire congregation is strengthened (Eph. 4:16). Equipping leads to service, which builds up the church and prepares the church to stand united against the Enemy.

Second, I am concerned that some churches give too little attention to their *goals* for doing ministry and service. Even when we minister to the needy, one of our goals ought to be to build them up for service. Ministry without follow-up usually promotes welfare and dependence rather than healthy Christian living.

For example, First Congregational Church provides a weekly meal at a homeless shelter as part of their ministry efforts in their community. This ministry is a needed one, but the church does little else to help the homeless. No one offers job skills training, though several church members could do so. Teachers in the church could provide literacy classes, but no one does. The shelter chaplain has requested mentors to disciple new believers, but no one has volunteered. No church member has yet offered employment to a homeless person.

My fear is that First Congregational believes their ministry responsibility is fulfilled, while their efforts may simply promote more dependence on the system. Healthy churches develop holistic ministry programs that offer mercy but also promote transformation and training. Love for their neighbors compels them to build up those to whom they minister. These churches produce discipled warriors rather than dependent ones.

Strategies of the Enemy

During the Vietnam War, Viet Cong fighters dug miles of underground tunnels for protection and secret transportation. Some tunnels were large enough to store tanks. So concealed were these tunnels that U.S. soldiers occasionally camped on top of a tunnel network, without any idea that the enemy they sought was under their feet.

That's how the Enemy battles ministry in the church. He disguises his schemes below the surface, subtly diverting energy from ministering to one another and to others. Sadly, the church does not always recognize his tactics until he has won. Generally, Satan's goal is to lead us to focus on ourselves. He promotes idolatry of self so that we neglect the needs of others, but how he does so is often not apparent. He tunnels beneath us.

The Enemy promotes arrogance.

Pride is a temptation for most of us, but we fail to admit the extent to which we struggle with ego. The following texts help us compare the weakness of pride with the strength of servant love:

> Text 1: "But you said in your heart, 'I will ascend to heaven; I will raise my throne above the stars of God, And I will sit on the mount of assembly In the recesses of the north. I will ascend above the heights of the clouds; I will make myself like the Most High." (Isa. 14:13–14)

> Text 2: "Have this attitude in yourselves which was also in Christ Jesus, who, although He existed in the form of God, did not regard equality with God a thing to be grasped, but emptied Himself, taking the form of a bond-servant, and being made in the likeness of men. Being found in appearance as a man, He humbled Himself by becoming obedient to the point of death, even death on a cross." (Phil. 2:5–8)

You probably recognize these passages as descriptions of Lucifer in text 1, a figure usually identified with Satan, and of Jesus in text 2. Lucifer sought glory, but Jesus walked away from it. Lucifer tried to ascend to the throne, but Jesus descended. One tried to become God, whereas the other willingly became human. The first wanted to be master, but the second took on the form of a slave. One was cast down for his pride. The other was exalted for His humility.

The personal pronoun *I* reverberates throughout the Isaiah 14 passage. Lucifer decided to "strive after self-exaltation, to assert his own position rather than to remain in position of service to God."[5] Arrogance captured his heart, and it led to his fall. The Enemy tries to lead believers to focus on themselves instead of others.

What does this strategy have to do with ministry through the church? People who focus on themselves take little time to minister to others. In many cases, they just don't minister at all.

Servanthood is for others who need purpose and meaning, not for those who already know how significant they are. In other cases, some minister only to gain attention. They want others to see how much they sacrifice and give. In either case, arrogance leads away from ministry that edifies people.

Pride also entices us to look down on others rather than build them up. One writer portrays Satan's whispered messages to prideful believers like this:

> You're all so vigilant! Always prepared, always on the defense against whatever I say. You know, if some of those other Christians seated around you on Sunday would just follow your example, your church would be positively on *fire* for God. But they're just so complacent, aren't they? . . . If I were you, I'd lay that list of lazy do-nothings before God in prayer and ask Him to *do* something about them! After all, it isn't fair! You spend all this time battling with me, and these people sit around on their . . .[6]

The Enemy tunnels beneath such arrogant people, even as they try to build their own kingdoms. He seduces them with power, knowing from his own experience that their pride ultimately will collapse on them (Prov. 16:18). In the meantime, he is pleased that their pride keeps them so focused on themselves that they choose not to minister to others.

The Enemy distracts with pain.

In John 5:2–9, Jesus confronted a lame man who had lain by the pool of Bethesda for many years. Each day he waited for healing, but no healing had occurred during almost forty years of sickness.

Strangely, Jesus asked him this question: "Do you wish to get well?" (v. 6). The man had been ill for thirty-eight years, and still Jesus asked the question. Why would He ask such a question? He knew that long-term pain often leads to discouragement and then to despair. Perhaps this man's heart had been paralyzed by so many years of pain, and Jesus' question was intended to jolt him out of his despair.

Jesus also knew that some people prefer to wallow in their pain rather than be healed. Pain brings attention from others. In a distorted way, continuing in the pain makes the person feel important. Perhaps Jesus was checking this man's heart with His question.

Do you see why the Enemy wants us to focus on our pain? If we live in despair, we have little joy to offer to a hurting world. Our emotional energy is sapped, and ministering to others seems physically and emotionally impossible. Some people even want to follow the advice of Job's wife and simply curse God and die (Job 2:9).

If we hang on to our pain for attention, *we* become the center of our world. We can become angry and jealous if other people get more attention. Might the Enemy, who himself essentially said, "I want all the attention" (Isa. 14:13), subtly promote this kind of attitude?

Meredith, a member of one of the churches I pastored, was convinced that the world was against her. She experienced recurrent health issues, and no doctor could meet her expectations. Years after her husband had divorced her, she used every opportunity to speak of the pain he caused her. When her young son was disobedient, she was sure he just wanted to hurt her.

Needless to say, Meredith was hardly interested in ministering to anyone else. And, to be honest, not many wanted to minister to Meredith for very long. Ministry halts when hurting people become self-centered and ministering people get burned out trying to help them.

The Enemy offers power without sacrifice.

How would you feel if you had just expressed your commitment to Jesus, and His response was, "Get behind Me, Satan! You are a stumbling block to Me"? Simon Peter must have felt great anguish when Jesus said those words to him after he had spoken against Jesus' coming death (Matt. 16:21–23). Peter loved Jesus, and he didn't want Him to die. Nevertheless, Jesus knew that the source of Peter's words was Satan, the same one who had offered Him the world earlier (Matt. 4:8–9). In both cases, the Enemy tried to entice Jesus to skip the cross. He could have the kingdoms of the world without dying, and He could please followers such as Peter, who saw no reason for Him to die. Ultimately, the Enemy offered Him a shortcut to power that required no sacrifice.

The problem, of course, was that God's will for Jesus demanded suffering and death. Had Jesus rejected the cross, there would have been no salvation for humanity (Heb. 9:22). This is why Jesus' response to Satan was so forceful and quick each time the offer was made. The Enemy's strategy still is to offer power and position without the trouble of taking up a cross daily to follow Jesus (Luke 9:23). He encourages people to seek the best seats in the kingdom because they believe they deserve them (see Matt. 23:5–7). Perhaps you've heard these voices of power without sacrifice:

- "I'm a founding member of this church, and I deserve to be a leader."
- "I give so much money to this church that you will close your doors without me."
- "My great-grandparents, my grandparents, and my parents were members of this church. I was here when you came, and I'll be here when you go."
- "It's your job, preacher, to do the ministry. We're just here to make sure you do it."

- "I may not always be faithful to the services, but I've not missed a business meeting in years!"

Few who express these kinds of attitudes, either in words or actions, ever do ministry. Genuine ministry demands humility and a servant's heart. It requires sacrifice. People who accept the Enemy's deals for power without sacrifice (see Exhibit 6-1) aren't willing to minister and serve other people.

Exhibit 6-1 Satan's Strategies and Suggestions for Power Without Sacrifice

Strategy . . .	Examples . . .
"Get an advocate to seek the position for you."	Matt. 20:20–21
"Build up yourself by tearing others down."	Luke 18:9–14
"Betray the leader (for a price)."	Luke 22:47–53
"Lie about your giving to the church."	Acts 5:1–11
"Brag about all the spiritual gifts you've received."	1 Cor. 12–14
"Teach what people want to hear. It doesn't have to be true."	2 Tim. 4:3–4
"Show partiality to those with wealth and power. They can be helpful friends."	James 2:1–4

The Enemy tempts to information idolatry.

Charles Spurgeon warned his ministerial students that every church is plagued with "certain Mrs. Grundys [who] are never quiet, but buzz around to the great annoyance of those who are devout and practical." In fact, Spurgeon wrote, "no one needs look far for perpetual motion, he has only to watch their tongues."[7]

The apostle Paul, too, warned against church members who "learn to be idle, as they go around from house to house; and not merely idle, but also gossips and busybodies, talking about things not proper to mention" (1 Tim. 5:13). Such a lifestyle characterized one who had "turned aside to follow Satan" (v. 15).

Think about the bait that the Enemy offered Eve in the Garden. "You will be like God, knowing good and evil," he said (Gen. 3:5). There apparently was (and is) something powerful about the promise of gaining knowledge, especially knowledge that someone else has but you do not. Knowledge gives us a sense of power and control. It is no wonder, then, that the writer of Proverbs describes the words of a gossip as "choice morsels" that stimulate a desire for more (Prov. 18:8 NIV).

Gossips are what I call "information idolaters." They seemingly cannot live without knowing everyone else's business. Whether they want to admit it, information becomes their god. Gossips typically hinder the overall ministry and service of the body by . . .

- revealing secrets (Prov. 11:13; 20:19). Who seeks help in a body whose members are not trustworthy?
- breaking relationships (Prov. 16:28). Broken fellowship weakens ministry.
- disrupting (1 Tim. 5:13). Leaders can spend so much time addressing the fallout of gossip that little time remains for legitimate ministry.
- tearing down. If a goal of ministry and service is edification, how can gossip do anything but hinder the church attempting to fulfill this purpose?
- undermining the work behind the scenes. They tear the body down, even as it attempts to build itself up. Gossips survive in the underground tunnels of the Enemy.

The Healthy Church Stands Armed

When an international force headed by the United States invaded Afghanistan in late 2001, strategists knew that mountain caves and tunnels would make their work difficult. They were better prepared to deal with this kind of warfare, though, because of what they had learned about tunnels during the Vietnam War. Christians also have enough experience and the help of Scripture that they can recognize the Enemy's schemes when he fights underground.

"Prayerwalk" your community.

Only when we really see people and their needs will we take seriously our mandate to minister. One simple way to begin to see people with God's eyes is to "prayerwalk" a community. Prayerwalking is simply walking through a community, praying for its people. Prayerwalkers might focus on factories and schools–wherever people with needs are. The goal of prayerwalking is to "pray onsite with insight," that is, to pray with more focus and intensity because we've seen the needs of the community.[8]

Troy Bush and his colleagues have the overwhelming task of developing a strategy to reach the fourteen million people of Moscow, Russia. The first step in their strategy is to prayerwalk the city, praying for each of the administrative districts. Missionaries, local church members, and American believers on short-term mission trips systematically walk and pray, asking God to open their eyes to opportunities. Several years ago, the missionaries discovered potential sites for church starts during a prayerwalk.

Think about some ways your church might reach its community through prayerwalking and ministry.

Exhibit 6-2 Prayerwalking and Ministering

If you see . . .	Pray . . .	Consider . . .
Children's toys on a lawn	that the children will be raised in a safe and godly home and will come to know the Lord as Savior.	offering child care personally (after earning the trust of the family) or through a "Parents' Night Out." Organize a block party.
A "for sale" sign	that those leaving will find a solid church and that the new owners might be a witness.	offering moving help or meals on moving day.
A school bus	that Christian teachers and administrators will have an impact, that children will be taught about God, and that they will be kept from harm.	volunteering at school, sending notes of thanks to teachers or bus drivers you know, or leading a "teacher's appreciation event" at church.
A person who is homeless or in known financial need	that this person will find the Lord, that you will know how best to help, and that ministry to the homeless will be effective.	providing food or clothing or helping the person contact social services.
A worship center for people whose faith is not in the true God and Christ as divine Savior	that the people there might hear the truth, that they might be led to genuine Christian friends, and that you might see people of that religion through God's eyes.	doing acts of kindness for someone in the group, offering friendship and sharing personal trust in Christ.

Lead in serving others.

Steve Sjogren, former pastor of the Vineyard Community Church in Cincinnati, Ohio, contends that believers take several approaches when they confront the darkness of the world. Some *evade* the darkness simply by withdrawing from the world. They avoid the darkness and are not inclined to evangelize people caught in darkness.

Other believers *pervade* the darkness by confronting it in the political, organizational, or spiritual realms. These evangelists try to run over the darkness.

Sjogren admits that there are times to evade and times to pervade, but he suggests that we usually should *invade* the darkness. *Invasion* occurs when we take light into the darkness by "demonstrating kindness in the power of the Holy Spirit,"[9] known as "servant evangelism."

Servant evangelism does simple acts of kindness as a potential open door to sharing the gospel. Servant evangelists might distribute free light bulbs, clean windows, rake leaves, shovel snow, or deliver meals. Their goal is to show God's love in action and perhaps gain a hearing for the gospel.

Several benefits accrue from servant evangelism:

1. *Servant evangelism projects require a church to look outward* and to move into the community. This counters our tendency to focus on ourselves.
2. *Servant evangelism is a low-risk way to get members involved in service.* People who aren't doing ministry aren't likely to make a commitment to a long-term, extensive responsibility. Servant evangelism is a step *toward* more extended commitments.
3. *Entire families can participate in servant evangelism projects.* Even preschoolers and children can help wash cars or distribute light bulbs. In fact, practical love expressed by children often melts the hearts of those living in darkness.

The following are the kinds of activities that make good servant evangelism projects. When undertaking such projects, always check possible liability and legal issues with an attorney:[10]

- Offer free soft drinks at local festivals. Note that food booths at such events fall under stringent health department regulation if food or open-container soft drinks are served.
- Collect food for the needy.
- Provide blood pressure screenings at a local mall.
- Feed expired parking meters, after checking to make sure that this does not violate a law or local ordinance.
- Wash outdoor windows.
- Wash cars.
- Provide free oil changes. Make certain first that this will not offend area mechanics and that legal oil disposal is available.
- Distribute batteries for smoke detectors.
- Provide umbrellas and escorts on a rainy day.

Minister through small groups.

Fellowship Bible Church of Little Rock, Arkansas, ministers extensively to its community throughout the city. Each year they coordinate "Sharefest," a community-wide ministry initiative. In 1999, more than one hundred churches and three thousand volunteers served Little Rock during Sharefest.[11]

Committed to being a church of "irresistible influence" in their community, Fellowship accomplishes its ministry through small groups. "Season of life" groups connect members who are at a specific life stage (e.g., young marrieds with children). "Common cause" groups are groups that study together and serve in a particular ministry. Fellowship's eighty common cause groups deal with such issues as substance abuse recovery, adoption services, tutoring, disaster relief, nursing home visitation, and sports outreach activities.

Small groups in any church provide a context for training, encouragement, accountability, and ministry. Especially as the church grows, small groups can easily become the ministering arm of the church. Rick Warren puts it thus: "The larger your church grows, the more important small groups become for handling pastoral care functions. They provide the personal touch that everyone needs, especially in a crisis. At Saddleback we like to say that the whole church is like a large ship, and the small groups are the lifeboat."[12]

Many Southern Baptist churches use "ministry group" or "care group" leaders in their Sunday education program classes to oversee ministry to members and guests. Each ministry group leader usually is responsible for an assigned group of six or eight members and guests. The group leader contacts group members each week, encourages their attendance on Sunday, remains alert to potential ministry needs, and coordinates appropriate responses when needs develop.

In a well-organized and healthy Sunday education program, ministry group leaders for every six to eight adults form quite a ministry force. Intentional ministry and service at the small group level helps produce a healthy church *and* alarm the Enemy.

Beyond the ministry component, consider other ways that small groups counter the Enemy's strategies:

- Small groups encourage healthy friendships, thus defending against the Enemy's aim to alienate (see chap. 8).
- A healthy small group ministry provides structure and direction. Disorganized bodies are vulnerable to the Schemer.
- Small groups can equip members to stand firm against the Enemy.
- Small groups provide accountability and prayer structure.
- Small groups promote corporate worship, keeping the people's eyes fixed on God.

Teach about grace.

As noted above (pp. 132–35), the Enemy works through both arrogance and pain to keep believers from ministering to others. Some members think that they are too significant to stoop to ministry; others are too wounded to believe that they have anything to offer. At either extreme the problem is an inward focus—pride. Counter the Enemy by teaching about grace.

We are saved through grace alone. The Ephesians 1–3 theological foundation in our healthy church model reminds us that we are saved only through God's grace (Eph. 2:8–9). We are in Christ solely because He has chosen to draw us into His kingdom.

Most evangelicals know this truth at the head level, but many live differently at the heart level. We believe in grace even while we try to show God and others just how important we are. The Enemy is pleased when we live in contrast to what we say we believe. A starting point to address this issue is to return to doctrinal teaching. Teach your church about radical human depravity and the grace of God. Believers who truly realize the depth of their need for God ought to lose their arrogance and be willing to minister to others.

We who have been saved by grace must offer grace to others. In 2 Corinthians 2:5–11, Paul urged the church to receive back into fellowship a brother who had been excommunicated. Although it is never stated, possibly this was the same man whose incest scandalized Paul in 1 Corinthians 5:1–5. Whoever he was, he had turned from his wrong and sought forgiveness. Paul challenged the church to forgive and comfort him. If they didn't receive him, sorrow might overwhelm him. Satan, who strives to create discord and division in the church, would have won the battle.

Paul expected the Corinthian believers to receive the man with grace. They who had been forgiven by grace must be gracious. The Enemy's footholds in a congregation are weakened when a church properly disciplines and then willingly welcomes again a repentant member.

Grace is always sufficient for our pain. The apostle Paul learned through a "thorn in the flesh, a messenger of Satan" that God's grace is sufficient (2 Cor. 12:7–10). The thorn weakened him, but God's strength became more and more real to Paul in his weakness. In the end, he proclaimed that he was well content with weaknesses and struggles that ultimately showed him the strength of God.

The Enemy dug his claws into Paul, but the deeper he dug, the more the apostle learned about grace. Rather than wallowing in pain to bring attention to himself, Paul rejoiced in his pain and directed the attention to God. Satan always loses when people in pain learn that God's grace is sufficient–regardless of whether He removes the pain.

We still need to direct struggling people to Paul's story. People who trust God in their pain often make the best ministers. They know the reality of the war, but they also can proclaim the joy of victory through God's grace. The healthy church teaches grace, lives grace, and offers grace. Discipled warriors never forget that the armor is theirs because of grace.

Application

The Enemy wars against ministry and service by leading believers to focus on themselves and to ignore the needs around them. Sometimes he is so subtle in his attacks that we don't even realize what is happening. He tunnels beneath us as we concentrate on our own lives above ground. Listen to the way Lord Foulgrin describes this strategy:

> Wrap them up in their jobs and houses and activities. . . . Keep their eyes on themselves, their programs, their buildings; never on the poor and needy and those who haven't heard the forbidden message. Keep their

> eyes on minivans and bank accounts and off the ends of the earth. . . . Turn their attention back to their favorite vacation spots, the big screen TV, the new car, the hot tub, the house they've been looking for out in the country.[13]

Churches resist the Enemy's attacks on their ministry and service by doing things like these:

- Study New Testament references to "one another."
- Preach and teach on the Great Commission and Great Commandment.
- Join other evangelical churches in cooperative community-wide ministry.
- Train or mentor members to minister in such difficult situations as death, illness, hospitalization, job loss, and depression.
- Organize servant evangelism projects.
- Study such resources as *His Heart, Our Hands,* a ministry evangelism guide published through the Southern Baptist Convention (see below).
- Challenge members to minister to the community "untouchables," whether homeless or in jail or victims of HIV.
- Conduct research into community ministry needs with direction from political leaders, school employees, and social workers. Determine steps your church might take to meet some of these needs.
- Prayerwalk. Challenge members to prayerwalk at school and at their workplaces.
- Take part in workplace ministry, for example serving as a volunteer chaplain at a local factory.
- Organize an international mission trip to minister to hurting people around the world.
- Study in groups what the Bible says about grace.
- Evaluate church equipping ministries and begin a more

aggressive and intentional approach to equipping for ministry.
- Arrange a "Great Day of Service" like the one described in this chapter.

For further study

Arnold, Jeffrey. *Starting Small Groups*. Nashville: Abingdon, 1997.

Berkeley, James D., ed. *Leadership Handbooks of Practical Theology: Outreach and Care*. Grand Rapids: Baker, 1994.

Callahan, Kennon. *Preaching Grace*. San Francisco: Jossey-Bass, 1999.

Dudley, Carl S. *Basic Steps Toward Community Ministry*. Washington, D.C.: Alban Institute, 1991.

George, Carl F. *Nine Keys to Effective Small Group Leadership*. Mansfield, Pa.: Kingdom, 1997.

Hemphill, Ken, and Bill Taylor. *Ten Best Practices to Make Your Sunday School Work*. Nashville: Lifeway, 2001.

His Heart, Our Hands. Alpharetta, Ga.: North American Mission Board, Southern Baptist Convention, 2000.

Keller, Timothy J. *Ministries of Mercy*. Phillipsburg, N.J.: Presbyterian and Reformed, 1997.

Martin, Glen, and Gary McIntosh. *Creating Community: Deeper Fellowship through Small Group Ministry*. Nashville: Broadman & Holman, 1997.

Payne, Bishop Claude E., and Hamilton Beazley. *Reclaiming the Great Commission: A Practical Model for Transforming Denominations and Congregations*. San Francisco: Jossey-Bass, 2000.

Shelley, Marshall, ed. *Building Your Church Through Counsel and Care*. Minneapolis: Bethany House, 1997.

Sjogren, Steve. *Conspiracy of Kindness*. Ann Arbor: Vine, 1995.

——. *Servant Warfare*. Ann Arbor: Vine, 1999.

Taking Prayer to the Streets. Alpharetta, Ga.: North American Mission Board, Southern Baptist Convention, 1999.

Zuck, Roy, ed. *Ministering to Twenty-first Century Families*. Dallas: Word, 2001.

Notes

1. See Donald A. Atkinson and Charles L. Roesel, *Meeting Needs, Sharing Christ* (Nashville: Lifeway, 1995).
2. "Ministry Evangelism," *SBCLife* (June/July 1998), 1–3.
3. Bob Russell with Rusty Russell, *When God Builds a Church* (West Monroe, La.: Howard, 2000), 216.
4. Atkinson and Roesel, *Meeting Needs*, 143.
5. Robert Dean Jr., and Thomas Ice, *What the Bible Teaches About Spiritual Warfare* (Grand Rapids: Kregel, 2000), 47.
6. Robert Don Hughes, *Satan's Whispers* (Nashville: Broadman, 1992), 143.
7. Charles Spurgeon, *Lectures to My Students* (Grand Rapids: Zondervan, 1954), 324.
8. Steve Hawthorne and Graham Kendrick, *Prayerwalking* (Orlando: Creation House, 1993), 15.
9. Steve Sjogren, *Servant Warfare* (Ann Arbor: Vine, 1996), 104; see also 96–98.
10. See Alvin Reid and David Wheeler, *Servanthood Evangelism* (Alpharetta, Ga.: North American Mission Board, Southern Baptist Convention, 1999), 26–29.
11. Robert Lewis, with Rob Wilkins, *The Church of Irresistible Influence* (Grand Rapids: Zondervan, 2001), 170.
12. Rick Warren, *The Purpose Driven Church* (Grand Rapids: Zondervan, 1995), 327.
13. Randy Alcorn, *Lord Foulgrin's Letters* (Sisters, Ore.: Multnomah, 2000), 258–59.

CHAPTER 7

Discipled Warriors Encountering God

Acts 2:42

Roberta's life was hardly victorious. She dated abusive men. Crack cocaine and alcohol controlled her life. She sold her furniture to support her drug habit. Periods of sobriety were brief.[1] Most people who knew Roberta had given up on her. She gave up on herself, especially after a blood test came back positive for HIV. What Roberta's family and friends could not have known, though, was that at one of her lowest points, Roberta would visit Brooklyn Tabernacle, a church known for its music and prayer. Every Tuesday night, members of the church fill the building beyond capacity for a time of prayer. Visitors come from around the world to attend this prayer meeting. Brooklyn Tabernacle also sponsors the "Prayer Band," a twenty-four-hour-a-day intercessory ministry.

Tabernacle members expect lives to be changed when they encounter God in prayer, just as Roberta was changed when she began worshiping with this congregation. Now she leads the church's outreach to drug abusers and the homeless. This church often sees such victory over Satan.

Our Calling to Pray

In chapter 1 (pp. 23–24), prayer is added to the usual list of five purposes for the church. Whereas most writers simply assume prayer within the other five purposes, I have elevated it to its own category. Let me explain why.

The early church prayed.

In the Acts 2:42–47 snapshot of life in the early church, the five purposes that most writers recognize are clearly evident:

1. *Worship.* "Everyone kept feeling a sense of awe; and many wonders and signs were taking place through the apostles. . . . Day by day . . . they were . . . praising God and having favor with all the people" (2:43, 46–47a).
2. *Evangelism.* "And the Lord was adding to their number day by day those who were being saved" (2:47b).
3. *Discipleship.* "They were continually devoting themselves to the apostles' teaching" (2:42).
4. *Ministry/service.* "And all those who had believed were together and had all things in common; and they began selling their property and possessions and were sharing them with all, as anyone might have need" (2:44–45).
5. *Fellowship.* "They were continually devoting themselves . . . to fellowship, to the breaking of bread. . . . they were taking their meals together with gladness and sincerity of heart" (2:42, 46).

Another aspect of the church's ministry is indicated in Acts 2:42, however: "They were continually devoting themselves to the apostles' teaching and to fellowship, to the breaking of bread *and to prayer*" (emphasis added). According to the Acts 2 description, prayer was a vital part of the church's life. Acts tells the story of believers who spent much time praying:

- "They all joined together constantly in prayer" (1:14 NIV).
- "Peter and John were going up to the temple at the time of prayer" (3:1 NIV).

- "After they prayed, the place where they were meeting was shaken" (4:31 NIV).
- "And [we] will give our attention to prayer and the ministry of the word" (6:4 NIV).
- "Peter went up on the roof to pray" (10:9 NIV).
- "But the church was earnestly praying to God for him" (12:5 NIV).
- "So after they had fasted and prayed, they placed their hands on them and sent them off" (13:3 NIV).
- "Paul and Barnabas . . . with prayer and fasting, committed them to the Lord" (14:23 NIV).
- "Paul and Silas were praying and singing hymns to God" (16:25 NIV).
- "When he [Paul] had said this, he knelt down with all of them and prayed" (20:36 NIV).
- "Paul went in to see him and, after prayer, placed his hands on him and healed him" (28:8 NIV).

Prayer was as much a part of the calling of the early church as were worship, evangelism, discipleship, ministry, and fellowship.

Scripture calls us to pray.

Actually, the Bible *assumes* that we will pray. Abraham interceded for the cities of Sodom and Gomorrah, and Lot was rescued (Gen. 18:20–33; 19:29). Moses talked to God (Exod. 3:1–4:17) and interceded for the children of God (32:11–13). Joshua discovered sin in the Hebrew camp through prayer (Josh. 7:6–26), but he also later failed miserably when he did not seek God's counsel (9:1–14).

David and Solomon sought the Lord's face for forgiveness and direction (e.g., 1 Kings 3:5–9; Psalm 51). Nehemiah sought his king's favor through prayer (Neh. 1:4–2:8). Daniel's commitment to prayer landed him in the lion's den, but God protected him there (Daniel 6). Jeremiah prayed with passion and honesty (Jer. 20:7–18).

Jesus, of course, prayed. He sought quiet places to pray (Luke 4:42; 5:16). He prayed in the morning (Mark 1:35), into the evening (Matt. 14:23), and through the night (Luke 6:12). He prayed before making major decisions (Matt. 26:36–46; Luke 6:12). He prayed during times of incredible struggle (Matt. 26:36–46; 27:45–46). He prayed passionately for His followers (John 17).

Prayers of thanksgiving and intercession echo through Paul's writings (e.g., Rom 1:8; 1 Cor. 1:4; Eph. 1:16; Phil 1:3–4; 1 Thess. 1:2–3). Paul considered prayer essential to continuing faithfully in the Christian life (Rom. 12:12), and he strongly encouraged prayer (Eph. 6:18; Phil. 4:6; Col. 4:2; 1 Tim. 2:1). Indeed, he expected believers to pray continually (1 Thess. 5:17).

While early believers needed direction in how to pray (Eph. 6:18–20; Col. 4:2; 1 Thess. 5:17; James 5:13–16), talking with God was as natural for them as a child's talking to a father (Rom. 8:15–17). Prayer was nonnegotiable in the life of their church—as it should be in today's church. God expects us to pray, and He expects us to grow healthy churches that focus on praying.

Strategies of the Enemy

When my wife and I married, I could not have imagined struggling to communicate with her. During our courtship, we usually spoke to each other several times a day. But we've learned through our years of marriage that communication doesn't come easily. When we are weak in this area, usually I am the problem. I have learned that I must work on communication if I want our love to be strong. I also must work on building our love if I want our communication to be strong. Relationship and communication cannot be separated in marriage.

The same is true of prayer. Believers must pray if we want a strong relationship with God, and we must have a healthy connection to Him if we expect our prayers to be effective.

The Enemy hits us at both levels. He leads us away from prayer so that our ties to God are weakened. And he strikes at our walk with God so that our prayer life is ineffective. Believers who fall to this double attack are not in a position to alarm Satan.

Christians are lured from prayer.

In C. S. Lewis's book *The Screwtape Letters*, the demon Screwtape tells his protégé Wormwood that he ought to keep the human being he is tempting "from the serious intention of praying altogether."[2] If prayer is given so much importance in the Scriptures, why wouldn't a believer pray?

First, our relationship with God is so anemic that talking with Him daily doesn't seem important. People in love are highly motivated to communicate with one another, whether in person, by telephone, or computer link. We find ways to express our love. If love begins to die, the efforts to communicate decrease proportionately. We stop talking when we stop loving. With God, prayer declines as love decreases. Needless to say, a healthy church loves God and so prays.

Second, we don't pray because we think we can get by without it. Consider Joshua's failure with the Gibeonites (Josh. 9). The Hebrews had followed God's orders at Jericho (chap. 6), and He had given them an amazing victory. They had done as God said in condemning Achan (chap. 7). But when the Gibeonites pretended that they were from a far-off country (see Deut. 20:10–18), the Hebrew leaders were taken in because they did not seek God's direction (Josh. 9:14). They determined on their own that the Gibeonites were telling the truth. On their own, they were easily misled. Too often, we depend upon ourselves and ignore what God thinks. Prayer is not important to us because we think we can survive on our own. The result is that the Enemy deceives us.

Third, consuming doubt keeps us from praying. Faith believes that God is and that He rewards those who seek Him (Heb. 11:6). If I doubt God's existence, concern, or ability to respond, why should I pray? If God fails to answer my prayers in the way I think He should, why trust His love? Why would a loving God delay to respond when I need a response *now*?

The Enemy is a master at producing doubt. His first recorded words in Genesis were, "Did God really say . . ." (3:1 NIV) as he sowed doubt in Eve's mind. Moses only records twice that Satan spoke to Eve, but she apparently fell quickly to his insinuations and misrepresentations and questioned God's motives and care. This Enemy wants us to doubt God so that we no longer pray to Him.

Prayer is made ineffective.

If the Enemy can't keep believers from praying, he seeks to lead us astray so that our prayers are ineffective. Primarily, he tempts us with sin, strikes at our relationships, or leads us to pray selfishly.

Satan tempts us to sin, so our prayers might not be heard. "Behold, the LORD's hand is not so short That it cannot save; Nor is His ear so dull That it cannot hear. But your iniquities have made a separation between you and your God, And your sins have hidden His face from you so that He does not hear." (Isa. 59:1–2). "If I regard wickedness in my heart, the Lord will not hear . . ." (Ps. 66:18).

Both the psalmist and Isaiah knew that God does not hear the prayers of those who persist in sin. It is the fervent prayer of a *righteous* man that makes a difference (James 5:16), not the prayers of one living in unrighteousness.

God gave Adam and Eve all of the Garden of Eden, with the exception of the tree of the knowledge of good and evil. He provided incredible blessings, but the serpent directed them *to the one thing God withheld* (Gen. 3:1–8). "You'll never know what you're missing," he implied. "In fact, God just wants to keep that from you so that you don't become like Him." Adam and Eve so focused on the forbidden tree that they no longer listened to God's voice. And when they broke His command, they found themselves hiding in terror instead of talking to Him.

This is how the Enemy works. He directs our attention away from God toward the *potential* pleasures of sin. We choose to give in to the temptation. Satan offers more and more pleasure until our prayer line is broken. Lost communication with God is the price we pay for continued sin–and the Enemy wins. That price is much too high for temporary pleasure.

Satan also aims at our interpersonal love. The apostle Peter told men to treat their wives with honor and respect "so that your prayers will not be hindered" (1 Peter 3:7). A husband who does not treat his wife well is not inclined to pray, nor can he pray effectively. The point of chapter 8 is that God uses our connections to each other so that we better understand His love for both us and others. The Enemy wants to destroy these relationships, and he wants the sin of broken love to sever our communion with God. For now, recognize that our connections with each other have much to do with our prayer life:

> He who shuts his ear to the cry of the poor Will also cry himself and not be answered. (Prov. 21:13)

> Therefore if you are presenting your offering at the altar, and there remember that your brother has something against you, leave your offering there before the altar and go; first be reconciled to your brother, and then come and present your offering. (Matt. 5:23–24)

> Whenever you stand praying, forgive, if you have anything against anyone, so that your Father who is in heaven will also forgive you your transgressions. (Mark 11:25)

> Therefore I want the men in every place to pray, lifting up holy hands, without wrath and dissension. (1 Tim. 2:8)

The Enemy leads us toward arrogant and selfish praying. Jesus condemned those who "love to stand and pray in the synagogues and on the street corners so that they may be seen by men" (Matt. 6:5). He illustrated this point with the parable of the Pharisee and the tax collector who were praying at the temple. The righteous Pharisee prayed out of his pride and was not heard, but the sinful tax collector humbled himself and was forgiven (Luke 18:10–14). Wayne Grudem reminds us that "God is rightly jealous for his own honor [and] therefore he is not pleased to answer the prayers of the proud who take honor to themselves rather than giving it to him."[3] Those who seek honor for themselves rather than for God—even in praying—sound dangerously like the Enemy.

Selfish ambition and desire for pleasure also mark the presence of the Enemy. Self-centered people pray "with wrong motives, so that you may spend it on your pleasures" (James. 4:3). Like the prodigal son, people ask for blessings that they fully intend to use for their own indulgence. Friendship with the world motivates their praying (Luke 15:11–32; James 4:4). God sees through that kind of praying.

Churches talk more about prayer than pray.

A group of U.S. believers joined Russian Christians for a prayer time in Moscow. Several hours later, the prayer meeting ended—after most of that time had been devoted to heartfelt prayer. The Americans went to teach the Russians about prayer, but it was the Russians who had much to teach.

Many churches *talk* much about prayer, but they don't really *pray*. The programs are there to teach prayer, but the passion to maintain prayer is woefully lacking. Subtly, many local bodies are lulled into prayerlessness. Healthy churches, on the other hand, are *genuinely* praying.

Early in his ministry at Ash Street Baptist Church near Atlanta, Georgia, Pastor Randy Cheek sensed that God was leading Ash Street to a more aggressive prayer life. "I developed a personal conviction and passion that one's prayer life must be more than several appointed times throughout the week," said the pastor. "Prayer is a constant attitude of the heart toward a dialogue with Him."

Over a few years, the church implemented new approaches to corporate prayer. In a beautiful room built specifically for the purpose of prayer, more than seventy prayer warriors participate in the church's ministry. Community members have opportunities to submit requests via a "Community Prayer Needs" mailbox. A prayer telephone line operates twenty-four hours a day. Rev. Cheek found the impact to be phenomenal: "Unity has prevailed at Ash Street. You have heard the familiar statement, 'The family that prays together, stays together.' The same is true with this church. Through this emphasis on prayer I have observed a church standing together on the power of the Body of Christ at prayer. The Wednesday night prayer service is now what it was intended to be–PRAYER."[4] The Ash Street congregation doesn't just talk about praying; they threaten the Enemy.

Exhibit 7-1 (p. 158) compares the tendencies of a ministry characterized by doing prayer as opposed to discussing it. Which set of statements describes your congregation?

The Healthy Church Stands Armed

Frequent, fervent prayer invigorates our friendship with God, reinforces our resolve to stand against the Enemy, and strengthens the local body of Christ. Prayer allows us to stay in touch with the Commander during intense battles.

Exhibit 7-1 Prayer-talking and Prayer-doing Churches

Churches that talk about prayer . . .	Churches that pray . . .
tell people to pray.	*teach* people to pray.
announce prayer meetings.	*pray* at prayer meetings.
preach about prayer.	*preach* about prayer and *pray* during preaching.
may have a *prayer list*.	*intentionally pray* through the prayer list.
may have a *prayer ministry* as one ministry among many.	have a *prayer ministry* that covers every other ministry.
have leaders who *talk* about prayer.	have leaders who *model* prayer.
seldom alarm the Enemy.	*most threaten* the Enemy.

Equip believers to resist temptation.

We know that our sin directly influences the effectiveness of our prayers. Most churches, in fact, rightly call people to turn from sin. What they don't often do, though, is give believers directions in *how* to overcome sin. If you want your church to be a church that prays effectively, teach your members how to resist temptation.

1. Be aware of patterns that make you susceptible to temptation. Are you with certain people? Do you go to particular places? Are you alone? Avoid patterns that make you vulnerable. Keep watching and praying so you don't fall into temptation (Matt. 26:41).

2. Daily pray that God would protect you from the Evil One (Matt. 6:13). Ask Him to give you the wisdom to submit to Him and the strength to resist the Devil (James 4:7).
3. Run to God when temptation occurs. The longer you linger at the Devil's offer, the more likely it is that you will fall.
4. Focus on God's goodness and blessings. When the Devil entices you to see what you're missing, remember the blessings of God. Take time to think about all that God has done for you.
5. Remember the consequences of sin. The Enemy makes sin look inviting, but the consequences are devastating. Think past the temporary pleasure to recognize the long-term pain of disobedience.
6. Be sure to thank God for protecting you when He has given you strength to defeat the Enemy.
7. Hold yourself accountable to another Christian, who will pray for you to experience victory over temptation.

Teach prayer.

Just after Jesus had finished praying one day, one of His disciples voiced their common request: "Lord, teach us to pray" (Luke 11:1). These men knew about prayer from the synagogue. They had seen and heard Jesus pray. They knew that there was a dimension of understanding that only He could give. How many Christians are just waiting for someone to *teach* them to pray? Even those who know something about prayer and have seen prayer modeled may be missing much. Teaching about prayer will accomplish at least three significant goals.

First, people learn more about God's gracious nature, strengthening their theological foundation. When we pray, we communicate with the Creator of the universe. He allows us to encounter Him without destroying us while we are in His presence. In fact, He delights when we come before Him as His children

(Rom. 8:15–16). Knowing God is the bedrock of a healthy church that wins spiritual warfare.

Second, thorough teaching gives patience when prayer seems to go unanswered. It is vastly helpful to recognize that apparent silence does not mean that God is absent or uncaring. Faith that overcomes the Enemy prays on even when it seems like Satan is winning.

Third, teaching about and leading the church to pray keeps the focus on God. Prayers of adoration put the attention on God. Prayers of confession remove obstacles between God and the believer. Thanksgiving recognizes God's love and provision. Supplication and intercessory prayers affirm our dependence. Proper focus on God always weakens the Enemy's influence.

Jesus began to teach prayer by giving a simple model (Matt. 6:9–13). This is especially helpful for new believers, and that period of excited infancy is the best time to learn. Guide new believers and new members to speak to God when their excitement and commitment levels are high. Teach them to pray when the concept of speaking to *God* is still beyond their comprehension.

Identify older believers who have retained their own fascination with prayer. These are potential prayer mentors. We, like the disciples, learn best when we have a model. By enlisting and releasing prayer mentors into ministry, your church will pass along a flame that erupts throughout the congregation.

Pray in families.

Prayer in church should begin with prayer in the home. Faithful parents take advantage of every opportunity to teach their children to follow God (Deut. 6:4–9), including teaching them to pray. Regrettably, few churches challenge and train parents to do so.

Family prayer begins with couples who pray together, but many couples struggle with sharing spiritual intimacy. Somehow, relating at a personal spiritual level is often more difficult than any other kind of intimacy. Doug Wendel, a Navigator staff member, suggests these beginning steps for couples:[5]

- Husbands have the responsibility to take the initiative. Wives should make the suggestion and let God move.
- Schedule prayer times on the calendar.
- Pray for brief time periods at first.
- Pray for things important to you, such as children, marriage, and unsaved loved ones.
- Keep variety by praying a portion of Scripture or singing.
- Take turns praying.
- Stick to the prayer time from week to week.

One of my favorite pictures, titled "Spiritual Warfare," shows a father kneeling at his son's bedside as the son sleeps. Dad is praying for his boy, likely asking God to protect him from the Enemy and draw him closer to Him. Perhaps the father is also praying that he will set a worthy example for his children. Whatever specific prayers might have been intended, the artist knew that parents fight for their children on their knees.

Parents should not only pray for their children, but they should also teach their children to pray. Parents are to raise their children "in the discipline and instruction of the Lord" (Eph. 6:4), a phrase that implies training in righteousness. Model prayer while teaching children to pray. Families might, for example, pray together as part of the "Lighthouses of Prayer" movement.[6] To make their homes a lighthouse of prayer for their neighborhoods, families invite other believing families to join them to pray for unreached neighbors. Prayerwalking in the community (see pp. 139–40) is another option for families who choose to pray together.

Pray in the workplace.

As noted in chapter 1 (p. 29–30), Paul instructed the Ephesians to live out their faith in their homes and places of employment (Eph. 6:5–9). The apostle spoke of slaves and masters, but the principles still apply. Christian employees and supervisors are to work for God's glory, knowing that each works for the same Master (v. 9). We are to work heartily for the Lord, waiting patiently for His reward (Col. 3:23–24). Our faithful service in the workplace becomes a witness to nonbelievers.

Believers who want to influence their workplace might seek to begin on-site prayer meetings. Gaining appropriate permission is important, and neglecting work to pray is unacceptable. Fellow believers might want to pray together before work, after work, or during lunch breaks. Consider using the guidelines for evangelistic prayer in chapter 4 (p. 98).

In September 1857, a single individual, Jeremiah Lanphier, called for a noonday prayer meeting in New York City. The movement started slowly, but workers soon gathered in noon prayer meetings in cities all over the nation. What became known as the Prayer Revival of 1857–59 resulted in as many as one million converts.[7] Might God be calling laypersons to this kind of prayer again? Such a movement might begin with one believer who prays in the workplace.

Be willing to attempt great things for God.

Henry Blackaby's popular study, *Experiencing God*, challenges believers and churches to accept God-sized tasks:

> Some people say, "God will never ask me to do something I can't do." I have come to the place in my life that, if the assignment I sense God is giving me is something that I know I can handle, I know it probably is *not* from God. The kind of assignments God gives in the Bible are always God-sized. They are always beyond what people can do because He wants to demonstrate His nature, His strength, His provision, and His kindness

> to His people and to a watching world. That is the only way the world will come to know Him.[8]

By definition, God-sized tasks are larger than any one believer or congregation. Such tasks cannot be accomplished apart from prayer.

At Ash Street Church in Atlanta (see p. 157), the members set aside a year during which they would pray that God "do something at Ash Street whereby no man can even attempt to take the credit for it happening in any way." Pastor Cheek wants his congregation to see "the mighty hand of God."[9] Ask God to give your church this kind of vision—and then pray.

Excursus: What About "Warfare Prayer"?

Some contemporary spiritual warfare leaders teach a system of "warfare prayer," that is, praying against high-ranking demons that rule over particular regions or territories. After prayer warriors identify the spirit over a given territory and then pray for that spirit's power to be broken, the area is considered ready to evangelize.

Daniel 10:10–21 is used to support this concept. Daniel had prayed, but a supernatural force known as the "prince of Persia" delayed the response. Only after the angel Michael intervened did Daniel receive his answer. Some believe that the "prince of Persia" was a demonic force assigned to the geographical region. Based on that assumption, warfare proponents try to identify territorial spirits and pray that their power might be broken.

We should be cautious about accepting such a theology of prayer. Whether or not Daniel refers to spirits who influence regions, we are given no mandate to name powers or pray against them. Daniel knew nothing about the spiritual battle until *after* Michael had intervened. This text cannot be read as a prescription for doing spiritual warfare in this fashion.

Some prayer warriors focus so much on discerning the Enemy that they unintentionally miss what God is doing. The message of Daniel 10:10–21 was given to comfort Daniel. The spiritual battle was real, but God did what was necessary to accomplish His will. We must be careful not to become so enamored of the Enemy's ways that we miss God's hand.

Application

In December 1941, U.S. naval and air forces were caught off guard when a Japanese force of more than 350 planes attacked the base at Pearl Harbor and nearby landing fields. Nineteen ships were disabled or sunk, hundreds of planes were destroyed, and more than twenty-three hundred American military personnel were killed.

Yet, what seemed to be a tremendous victory turned out to have been a strategic failure. The submarine fleet and three Pacific fleet aircraft carriers were not at Pearl Harbor on December 7. The Japanese chose not to attack fuel depots and support facilities, so some battleships were repaired quickly. The enemy had hit hard, but they had not shut down the power of the United States.

Our spiritual Enemy hits hard, too. His strategy seldom fails to target our power supply—our prayer life. Healthy, prepared churches stand armed and so are not caught off guard. The following suggestions can strengthen that military readiness:

- Choose a prayer coordinator to oversee a prayer ministry that undergirds all ministries of the church.
- Preach on prayer as it is taught in the Bible. The book of Acts is a good starting point.
- Form prayer teams who consistently pray for each of the six purposes. For example, one prayer team concentrates on worship, and another on evangelism.
- Offer training seminars to teach people to pray.

- Sponsor quarterly prayer breakfasts or lunches for time focused on praying.
- Form accountability groups to hold each other accountable to pray.
- Seek members who can talk about the influence of prayer in their homes when they were children. Such stories encourage household prayer.
- Organize a church prayer chain that is activated daily—not only when emergencies arise. Train participants so that the chain does not become a gossip line.
- Plan a short-term mission trip built around prayerwalking in another country.
- Enlist prayer leaders in each Bible study class or small group to pray specifically for their leaders and outreach.
- Set aside the period between Mother's Day and Father's Day for daily prayer for families. Seek resources to help guide praying.
- Begin a weekly noon prayer time. Use it as a springboard to encourage participants to begin a meeting at work.
- Lead a study on the "theology of prayer." Seek to answer such questions as "Why doesn't God answer my prayers?"
- Do "focus on the family" praying, highlighting particular families each week. Pray corporately for *each* church family at least once during the year.

For further study

Bright, Bill. *The Transforming Power of Fasting and Prayer*. Orlando, Fla.: NewLife, 1997.

Floyd, Ronnie. *The Power of Prayer and Fasting*. Nashville: Broadman & Holman, 1997.

Franklin, John. *A House of Prayer: Prayer Ministries in Your Church*. Nashville: Lifeway, 1999.

Frizzell, Gregory. *Biblical Patterns for Powerful Church Prayer Meetings*. Master Design, 2000.

Hawthorne, Steve, and Graham Kendrick. *Prayerwalking*. Orlando, Fla.: Creation House, 1993.

Kamstra, Douglas A. *The Praying Church Idea Book*. Grand Rapids: Faith Alive, 2001.

Lee, Victor, and Jerry Pipes. *Family to Family: Families Making a Difference*. Alpharetta, Ga: North American Mission Board, Southern Baptist Convention, 1999.

Martin, Glen, and Dian Ginter. *PowerHouse: A Step-by-Step Guide to Building a Church that Prays*. Nashville: Broadman & Holman, 1994.

Murray, Andrew. *The Ministry of Intercessory Prayer*. Minneapolis: Bethany House, 1981.

Pederson, Bjorn. *Establishing a Prayer Ministry*. Minneapolis: Augsburg, 1995.

Piper, John. *A Hunger for God*. Wheaton, Ill.: Crossway, 1997.

Schofield, Chris. *Praying Your Friends to Christ*. Alpharetta, Ga: North American Mission Board, Southern Baptist Convention, 1999.

Tekyl, Terry. *Making Room to Pray*. Anderson, Ind.: Bristol, 1999.

——. *Your Pastor: Preyed on or Prayed For*. Anderson, Ind.: Bristol, 2000.

Vander Griend, Alvin J. *The Praying Church Sourcebook*. Grand Rapids: Church Development Resources, 1997.

Notes

1. Jim Cymbala, *Fresh Wind, Fresh Fire* (Grand Rapids: Zondervan, 1997), 40–46.
2. C. S. Lewis, *The Screwtape Letters* (Old Tappan, N.J.: Revell, 1976), 33.
3. Wayne Grudem, *Systematic Theology* (Grand Rapids: Zondervan, 1994), 386.
4. Randy Cheek, personal correspondence, December 2001.
5. Doug Wendel, "How to Get Started and Keep Going," *Pray!* 9 (November–December 1998): 29.
6. Cornell Haan, *The Lighthouse Movement Handbook* (Salem, Ore: Multnomah, 1999).

7. "Prayer Meeting Revival (1857–59)," *Dictionary of Christianity in America* (Downers Grove, Ill.: InterVarsity, 1990), 922.
8. Henry Blackaby and Claude V. King, *Experiencing God* (Nashville: Broadman & Holman, 1994), 220.
9. Cheek, personal correspondence, December 2001.

CHAPTER 8

Discipled Warriors Encouraging One Another

Acts 2:42, 46

Sandy and Carol were best friends. Their husbands were brothers, and Sandy's husband introduced Carol's family to Christ. They laughed together, traveled together, worshiped together, and prayed together–until Sandy and Carol found themselves at odds over whether the church should keep an ineffective youth minister. Sandy and her family stood by the young man, but Carol's family agreed with those who thought that a change was needed. In the end, the church dismissed the staff member and hired another young man whose passion for young people ignited the ministry. Sandy and Carol, though, never recovered their personal friendship. They avoid one another. Their husbands seldom speak. Family get-togethers are tense. Somehow, a God-honoring kinship turned sour.

Might the Enemy be involved in this situation? Satan works to create disunity in which God's foot soldiers shoot their own comrades in the back. An army at war within offers little danger to its Enemy.

Our Calling to Encourage Through Fellowship

I went to my first "church fellowship" at age thirteen, when I had been a Christian for only a few months. I had never even heard the term *fellowship* before the previous Sunday, when the word appeared in our bulletin. That Wednesday night I discovered that a "fellowship" was about eating . . . and eating . . . and eating some more. Some of the best cooks around were in that congregation, and I looked forward to the next time we would have "fellowship."

Several months later, I missed attending worship for several consecutive Sundays. A concerned member called to remind me that I needed to come. "The Bible tells us not to forsake the assembling of yourselves together" (Heb. 10:25), he warned. "Plus, you just need *fellowship* in the church in order to live faithfully."

I knew I needed to attend church, but I was not sure how eating would help me to live more faithfully. Needless to say, I was confused about the nature and purpose of true Christian fellowship—as are many believers today.

Support one another.

The early Christians "were continually devoting themselves to the apostles' teaching and to fellowship" (Acts 2:42). These believers committed themselves to *koinonia,* meaning "fellowship or a close relationship or association." Literally, the word suggests that the church members shared all things in common (2:44).

The church supported one another by distributing their material goods to those in need (2:44–45). They also met in homes for common meals (2:42, 46). The young Christian community shared life together, sustaining one another as the body of Christ. Although the church did not remain so united, those early believers provided a support system where, as John P. Newport described it, "joys are shared and burdens are borne."[1]

Support in the church is not limited to sharing goods and meals, however. True fellowship is in evidence when all believers rejoice that one member is honored, and all believers suffer if one member is hurting (1 Cor. 12:26). Believers truly bear one another's burdens (Gal. 6:2). At this level of unity, no individual is insignificant–and, no individual faces spiritual battles alone. Facing the Enemy is never easy, but knowing that we have the support of other believers ought to give us courage.

Build up one another.

Theologian Millard Erickson contends that fellowship is one means by which the church is edified in faith.[2] In genuine fellowship, believers strive to build each other up rather than tear each other down. This is clear in Paul's commands about building up the body of Christ. Paul never separates edification from the fellowship of Christian love:

> So then we pursue the things which make for peace and the building up of one another. (Rom. 14:19)

> Each of us is to please his neighbor for his good, to his edification. (Rom. 15:2)

> Speaking the truth in love, we are to grow up in all aspects into Him who is the head, even Christ, from whom the whole body, being fitted and held together by what every joint supplies, according to the proper working of each individual part, causes the growth of the body for the building up of itself in love. (Eph. 4:15–16)

> Let no unwholesome word proceed from your mouth, but only such a word as is good for edification according to the need of the moment, so that it will give grace to those who hear. (Eph. 4:29)

> Therefore encourage one another and build up one another, just as you also are doing. (1 Thess. 5:11)

One of the goals of a healthy church is to "present every man complete in Christ" (Col. 1:28), and genuine fellowship leads toward that goal. Believers who are affirmed, encouraged, loved, and supported are much more likely to march forward in Christian faithfulness when the Enemy strikes.

However, genuine fellowship does not imply that the church should never take disciplinary sanction against wayward members. As in the case of the Corinthian who was caught up in incest (1 Cor. 5:1–5; 2 Cor. 2:1–11), sometimes the most edifying action for the entire body is judgment intended to lead a member toward "restoration (of the offender to right behavior) and reconciliation (between believers, and with God)."[3] Effective disciplinary steps can strengthen a church's fellowship rather than disrupt it—and thereby weaken the Enemy's influence.

Encourage love and good deeds.

When the Christian brother used Hebrews 10:25 in calling me to task for not attending worship, he was right to tell me that I needed to come. I am not sure, however, that he fully understood the teaching of the text. This verse says much more than "You need to be with us." In the previous verses, the writer called believers to "hold fast" and to "stimulate one another to love and good deeds" (vv. 23–24). This is a call to hold one another accountable in Christian living, particularly in light of a coming day of judgment (v. 25).

One of the reasons early Christians met together was to prod each other toward faithful Christian living, especially when they faced persecution (see Heb. 10:32–39; 12:4). Believers who neglected the gatherings missed opportunities to receive support and motivation. They faced great danger if they continued to live apart from Christian encouragement and accountability.

True fellowship is about exhorting brothers and sisters to

persevere in faith. Exhortation and encouragement from fellow believers are especially important when we are under spiritual attack.

Brad is a Christian for whom genuine fellowship made a difference. He became a believer as a teenager but made immoral choices in his mid-thirties. His pastor and deacons loved him enough to confront him, informing him that the church would take action against him if he ignored their interventions. This awakened Brad to the seriousness of his situation. He returned to the church, publicly sought forgiveness, and agreed to be held accountable. Today he is a faithful Christian who is supported and daily encouraged to stay faithful. *That* is genuine fellowship–the kind that alarms the Enemy and against which he aims his arrows.

Strategies of the Enemy

Fellowship is about relationships. Consequently, most strategies the Enemy uses against genuine Christian fellowship strike directly at our interpersonal connections. He seeks to wound relations among Christians in general, and he is not much threatened by people who are self-centered and unconcerned about others.

The Enemy distorts relationships.

We have seen that distorted love, especially between spouses, affects our prayer (see p. 155). Healthy relationships, on the other hand, help us to understand the nature of God's love:

- Healthy marriages teach sacrificial, giving, unashamed love.
- Healthy parenting shows unconditional love that includes nurturing discipline.
- Healthy trust of children for parents teaches them to trust and love others who always have our best interests at heart.

- Healthy friendships show affirming, supportive, and even confrontational love.

Unhealthy relations make it difficult to understand or trust God's love. People who have been abused by an earthly father, for example, struggle to see the blessing of God's loving fathering. Those who have suffered in an abusive, unloving marriage can miss the beauty of the "bride of Christ" imagery in Ephesians 5. That doesn't mean we should ignore or change these biblical images. We should recognize, though, that some people's ideas about God reflect past scars.

If unhealthy affections make it more difficult to trust God, it stands to reason that the Enemy will promote situations that disrupt interpersonal ties and wound people.

Exhibit 8-1 describes Satan's efforts to distort relationships to his own ends. More on this important topic later in this chapter.

Exhibit 8-1 The Distortion of Relationships

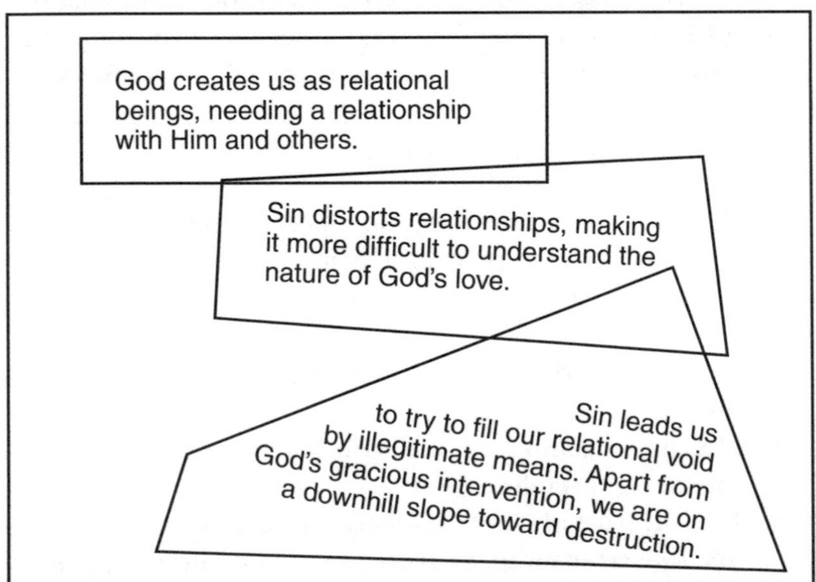

The Enemy divides believers.

The body of Christ is diverse, made up of many distinct parts, yet united in purpose and mission (1 Cor. 12:14). That very unity—the kind that only God can produce supernaturally—is a witness to a world that is chaotic and disjointed. No wonder Jesus prayed three times in His priestly prayer for His followers to be united (John 17:20–23).

In contrast, Satan promotes division. You'll recall that Adam blamed both God and his wife for his wrong (Gen. 3:11–12). Sin quickly drove a wedge between the first couple. Later, one of their children killed the other (Gen. 4:1–8), an indication of brokenness. Division has been a problem ever since. The church's witness often has been weak because members spend more time battling one another than they do standing firm against the Enemy.

The Enemy divides churches with no vision.

In many cases, Satan has to do little work to create disunity in a church. The disunity is often already there, particularly when the church has no unifying vision or direction. There is no known great cause driving the church forward, so they become inwardly focused and susceptible to division.

I describe this kind of church as a "reactionary" church, as opposed to an "expectant" church (see Exhibit 8-2). They have no marching orders, so the best they can do is to react to whatever comes their way. The Enemy typically finds this type of church to be less than a formidable foe. On the other hand, the healthy church is united around a vision, prayerfully expecting God to do His work through their church.

The Enemy takes advantage of bitterness.

Matthew 6:14–15 is a challenging text. Jesus told us that we cannot receive the Father's forgiveness for our sin unless we have

Exhibit 8-2 Expectant vs. Reactionary Churches

Expectant Churches . . .	Reactionary Churches . . .
have a *clear* sense of vision.	have *no known* vision.
seek God's face *before* a problem arises.	ask for God's help *after* a problem becomes serious.
have leaders who are *ignitors.* They light a passion for God.	have leaders who are *firemen.* They put out troublesome fires.
are *outward* focused.	are *inward* focused.
assume that God will build the body.	*feel surprised and sometimes threatened* by growth.
are characterized by *unity.*	are characterized by *division.*
are *armed targets* for the Enemy. They are targets but ready.	are *easy targets* for the Enemy.

forgiven those who have harmed or offended us. Hanging on to bitterness, we experience both the continued pain and the anguish of knowing that God is not pleased with our attitude.

Why does the Enemy so often succeed in rendering our spiritual lives unhealthy through bitterness? For one reason, many people have difficult pasts that have left some significant scars and pain. Bitterness is sometimes all these people have known, and they have never been helped to deal with the past. Those who grew up in abusive and/or broken homes are especially vulnerable.

In addition, our "victim" culture prefers to blame someone else for our own failures. If I actually forgive the people who messed up my life, then I must grow up and take responsibility for my actions. It is easier and more ego lifting to stay angry and unforgiving—and weak.

Bitter people gather in our midst at every worship service. Sometimes they lead the worship. Regardless of the source of their pain, unforgiving members ultimately weaken the entire body. Their bitter spirit is evident in the suspicion and hostility with which they react to those around them. The Enemy's seeds of division have already been planted in a church where members hold on to bitterness.

The Enemy encourages "koinonitis."

Satan typically wants to disrupt Christian fellowship, but occasionally he accomplishes his goals when there is *too much* fellowship. Congregations infected with "koinonitis" are so happy with their family atmosphere that outsiders are seldom welcome.[4] People see little reason to change anything, and they don't want growth to upset their fellowship.

"Christian cocooning" is both a cause and a result of koinonitis. Church members suffering from cocooning have become so involved in the church world that they no longer know any unchurched people. In contrast to God's willingness to interact with a lost world (Gal. 4:4–5), cocooned believers retreat to the fortress. There they develop koinonitis and almost dare outsiders to try to enter their world.

A simple exercise can determine if you and your church have developed either of these diseases. On a sheet of paper, write two lists of names. The first list should include the names of ten believers with whom you are close enough to share a prayer concern. The second list should include the names of ten nonbelievers with whom you are close enough to share the gospel. If the second list is much more difficult to complete, you probably have become cocooned. If many members discover the same reality, your body suffers from koinonitis and cocooning. While the church is obsessed with its time together, the Enemy watches without much concern.

In some sanctuaries or auditoriums, everyone has a personal

pew or chair. Everybody knows everybody else, and nobody wants to upset their sweet fellowship. I once preached in a building where the front door remained locked during all gatherings because "Everybody around here knows we come in the back door." Do you suppose the Enemy was too bothered by this congregation's outreach attitude?

The Healthy Church Stands Armed

Not far from the seminary where I teach is a military base. Soldiers billeted there have been deployed in several conflicts. When the troops depart, local media always interview family members. The emotions usually are gut wrenching, but I've noticed that families gain strength from other families. They support each other as their husbands and fathers are in harm's way. They know they can depend on one another.

The healthy church that wins spiritual battles has such a support system. Genuine fellowship edifies and strengthens for the battle.

Promote love and good works.

I doubt that many churches will easily change the concept that "fellowship" is about having fun and eating together. I'm not sure we should change that concept entirely, for fellowship in the early church did include sharing and eating together. Yet, think about the *many* "fellowship" events at churches and consider how strongly they promote love and good works (Heb. 10:24). Most of these events, such as small group gatherings, recreational events, and holiday celebrations, almost unintentionally promote love and good works. Just being together for fun and celebration allows us to enjoy our faith.

Nevertheless, a few simple strategies might help the church to grow stronger through these events:

- At dinners, enlist one or two brief testimonies that will spur on others.
- Use recreation for intentional outreach. Organize events to which unbelieving friends and relatives can be invited.
- Promote mutual accountability through small groups. Hold each other to high standards.
- Prepare and deliver meals for hurting and unchurched neighbors.
- At holiday times, add an event for those who find it difficult to celebrate. Small groups might, for example, visit nursing homes or prisons. Plan ahead for jail and prison events. They can be valuable, but rules are strict, and gaining proper security clearances is often time consuming. States often require advance training.
- Read Scripture at all gatherings. Choose texts that are clear, concise, yet challenging. Let the Bible provoke members to good works.
- Fellowship around ministry events. For instance, an evangelistic block party is a great opportunity to fellowship with believers while reaching nonbelievers. Keep the focus outward even as you enjoy each other.
- When evaluating events, consider whether they intentionally promote love and good works.

Promote unity.

The citizens of Feldkirch, Austria, were under siege by Napoleon on Easter in 1799. Close to surrender, the people gathered around their bishop, who called them to celebrate the Lord's resurrection day by ringing all the church bells of the village. Enemy forces heard the bells ringing throughout the town. They concluded that the Austrian army was coming to raise the siege. Soon after the bells stopped ringing, Napoleon's forces already were withdrawing.

Something like that happens when God's people join forces. No matter how strong the Enemy, he is no match for a praying, united body of believers. No wonder Paul warned the church to work together and to beware of divisive people (Rom. 16:17; 1 Cor. 1:10; Titus 3:10). The healthy church overcomes the Enemy by battling from a united front (see Eph. 2:11–22; 4:1–16).

Lead members to forgive.

As a consultant for a church that had split many years before from a sister church two miles away, I easily identified which members had been involved in the division. They talked a little louder, turned red in the face, and quickly gave their perspective on what had happened almost twenty years earlier. Their anger had not subsided. Unresolved anger gives the Devil an opportunity to spread his influence, even when that anger remains hidden. Warfare writers Neil Anderson and Charles Mylander describe this danger and its remedy:

> Those who do not understand the forgiveness and the power of praying for past offenders sometimes refuse to face old painful memories. They delude themselves and fall into the devil's trap. Some of Satan's favorite deceptions are that darkness is safer than light, that things hidden are better not discussed, that pain has no permanent resolution. . . . Wise church leaders bring everything into the light. . . . They claim God's grace to release them from the bondage of the past. They feel the pain, release it through the forgiveness of Christ, and bless those who curse them.[5]

Genuine Christian fellowship does not occur if church members are holding on to yesterday's pain, whether that pain is individual or corporate. Forgiving others who have wounded us is seldom easy, but it is necessary if we want to grow churches that honor God and overcome the Enemy. Discipled warriors are forgiving warriors.

Challenge the people who need to forgive someone to let go of their bitterness (see Exhibit 8-3). Perhaps these evaluative questions and possible responses will help you accomplish this imperative task.

Exhibit 8-3 The Challenge to Forgive

Enemy Strategy: Promote Bitterness and an Unforgiving Heart.

Evaluation: Do I need to forgive?	**Response: What should I do to forgive?**
1. Do I dwell on the pain?	Focus on God's forgiveness of your sins (Luke 7:40–50).
2. Do I avoid dealing with the issues?	In an appropriate setting, admit anger. Bringing it into the light weakens the Enemy's hold (John 8:32).
3. Do I want the offender to hurt before I forgive?	Determine to forgive, even if you do not feel like it. Ask God for the heart of Jesus (Luke 23:34) and Stephen (Acts 7:60).
4. Do I have physical symptoms (e.g., stomach distress, headaches, eating disorders) when I think about the pain?	Ask God to give you His incomprehensible peace (Phil. 4:7).
5. Can I rejoice if God blesses the one who hurt me?	Pray for the person (Matt. 5:44).

Forgiveness breaks the Enemy's stranglehold.

Promote reconciliation and unity in the community.

The Church at Modesto is an umbrella name for an organization of congregations in Modesto, California. Leaders and members have covenanted together to "shepherd the city" in prayer, demonstrating love, pursuing reconciliation, meeting community needs, and proclaiming the gospel.[6] Each week, more than one hundred members from fifty or sixty churches gather to pray for the city. "Lighthouses of prayer" exist throughout the community. A youth center is planned. A police chaplaincy has been established. Pastors throughout the city use a common marriage covenant when counseling engaged couples.

Might this kind of intentional unity weaken the Enemy's hold in a city? Without compromising the essentials of the gospel, challenge your church to promote and support Christian unity in your city. What might happen if believers around your community united in fellowship and continuously encouraged one another to love and good works? Satan's flaming arrows of division would be deflected, if not extinguished completely.

Nurture healthy relationships.

As was noted in Exhibit 8-1 (p. 174), the Enemy works to distort what we feel for each other, and the church's responsibility is to promote healthy relationships. Most of the time, however, churches do little to promote deeper love. We just assume that people understand what it takes to build a strong friendship. The Bible corrects our thinking by stressing how to love and relate. For example, . . .

- "For this reason a man shall leave his father and his mother, and be joined to his wife; and they shall become one flesh" (Gen. 2:24).
- "Honor your father and your mother" (Exod. 20:12).
- "A friend loves at all times" (Prov. 17:17).

- "Do not forsake your own friend or your father's friend" (Prov. 27:10).
- "The husband must fulfill his duty to his wife, and likewise also the wife to her husband" (1 Cor. 7:3).
- "Husbands, love your wives, just as Christ also loved the church and gave Himself up for her" (Eph. 5:25).
- "Do nothing from selfishness or empty conceit" (Phil. 2:3).
- "Children, be obedient to your parents in all things, for this is well-pleasing to the Lord" (Col. 3:20).
- "Masters, grant to your slaves justice and fairness, knowing that you too have a Master in heaven" (Col. 4:1).

Given the fact that the Bible so clearly guides us in developing Christian and family love, why have one-third of confessing evangelicals experienced divorce? Why have 25 percent of apparently born-again Christians lived together with someone outside marriage?[7] Why did the percentage of single-parent families more than triple between 1960 and 1998? Why are the odds one in two that a child will witness his parents' breakup?[8]

Former U.S. Secretary of Education William Bennett argues that such problems arise from a shift in fundamental values, sexual revolution, new rules regarding male-female relationships, participation of women in the workplace, popular culture's influence, and other complex social dynamics.[9] I would add another reason for the relational disengagement: The church simply has not done a good job of teaching biblical principles for relating to each other. No wonder churches are often in turmoil. People who have not learned to relate to others struggle with the relationships in congregational life.

Healthy churches teach, promote, and model love. These churches equip couples to be good spouses. They train parents to be good parents. They challenge young people to be respectful and obedient. They show neighbors how to be good neighbors, and friends how to be true friends. As connections are nurtured, fellowship among believers grows strong. Exhibit 8-4 stresses the need to build healthy relationships to counter the Enemy's strategies.

Get outside of the church walls.

Churches that overcome the Enemy must counter koinonitis and cocooning. What do you do when the people lose their outward focus? There are at least four options:

1. Ignore the issue. Just keep members happily looking at themselves.
2. Preach that the church must look outward but give no strategy for moving into the world.
3. Devise a strategy for moving beyond the cocoon but do not support the initiative with strong teaching.
4. Preach that the church must focus outward *and* offer a specific strategy for doing so.

Option 1 is unacceptable because each congregation is called by the Great Commission to reach the world (Matt. 28:18–20). Option 2 is incomplete—not because preaching the Word is too weak to move people, but because the Word itself reveals a God who leads by a plan (e.g., Exodus 25–31; Luke 10:1–12; Acts 1:8). Option 3 provides the strategy but provides no theological support for implementation; hence, biblical motivation to continue will be weaker.

Option 4, the best approach of preaching, hearing, and doing demands a *vision* and a plan. Show why the congregation must move beyond itself, then equip them to do so. Provide opportunities, such as servant or ministry evangelism. Raise up discipled warriors to take the light of the gospel into the darkness, and koinonitis and cocooning are much less likely to occur.

Exhibit 8-4 Relationships in the Christian Life

Design	Distortion	Results of Distortion	God's Answers
God made us to relate to Him. His love is reflected in relationships with others (Gen. 2:18). Relationships help us understand God's love: • Spouse—committed, sacrificing love. • Parent-child—love that sacrifices and does not have conditions. Disciplining. • Friend—Unexpected, forgiving love.	Satan distorts God's plan, knowing that poor human relationships do not reflect God's love toward us and others. Examples of distortions: • abuse • blame • anger • bitterness • fear • divorce • idolatry • promiscuity • selfishness	*Ignoring* relationships in fear of commitment and self-sufficiency leads to isolation and sin as we try to fill void (e.g., pornography). *Imitating* true relationships with false ones doesn't meet needs and causes pain. *Idolizing* relationships out of fear of loss and perceived inadequacy leads to controlling codependency. The result is trouble in trusting the love of God or others.	Find again the truth of His love in renewed relation. • In marriage we learn sacrifice. • With parents and children, we learn love that respects and doesn't give up. • In church we learn to value one another. • In friends, we learn God's love for others and how to serve Him. Legitimate, godly relationships fill the need designed in us. Anything less leads only to sin.
The need for relationships is a gift. This is an important part of life.	**Satan wants to destroy relationships, weakening their witness.**	**We try to fill proper needs by illegitimate means. We live selfishly as we try to fill unmet needs.**	**God gives people to us that we might know His love. The church helps believers experience this blessing.**

Application

It was only a drama on television, but the story line was all too real. The husband of one of the main characters had been deployed to defend his country in war. His wife worried continually that their love would not be the same when he returned—*if he returned.* Would he still love her? Would their infant recognize Daddy?

The fears proved unfounded, but real life can be messier. Solid affections can change under the tension of separation and fear. In fact, the stresses of daily life can hurt relationships.

Sadly, relationships sometimes are a casualty of the spiritual war we're fighting. The healthy church must intentionally develop strong Christian connections to ward off the Enemy's attacks. Consider the following fellowship-building suggestions:

- Enlist a Christian counselor to teach a seminar on biblical principles of forgiveness.
- Preach on what the Bible says about fellowship.
- Assign a mature believer to pray for and support each new believer. Be intentional in promoting mentoring, accountable friendships that encourage.
- Sponsor a quarterly or monthly community-wide prayer service. Recruit as many pastors to participate as possible.
- Write notes to encourage faithful workers.
- Creatively arrange fellowship events that encourage love and good works.
- Find people who can share testimonies of how God has used others in their walks with Christ.
- Contract with a highly competent Christian counselor to provide marriage and other counseling services at a reduced rate. This service can open doors to the unchurched.
- Plan monthly or quarterly staff meetings that build a team attitude among leaders and active workers. Those involved with the separate ministries can encourage each other.

- Lead a study on relationship principles in the Bible.
- With leaders (and perhaps others in the congregation) take the cocooning test (see p. 177).
- Do an exit survey of visitors. Find out if the church is friendly to outsiders. Share the results with members, devising a strategy to correct weaknesses.
- Enlist longer-term members to review your church's history. Look for past wounds that still affect the church.
- Conduct dating, marriage, and parenting seminars.
- Mobilize an "e-mail encouragement team" who is responsible for e-mailing encouraging messages to different church members each week.
- Design an assimilation strategy to move new members into a small group quickly. Teach each small group leader that one of his or her responsibilities is to prod believers to love others and to do good works.

For further study

Allender, Dan, and Tremper Longman III. *Bold Love*. Colorado Springs: NavPress, 1992.

Augsburger, David. *Caring Enough to Confront*. Glendale, Calif.: Regal, 1980.

Barna, George. *The Power of Team Leadership*. Colorado Springs, Col.: Waterbrook, 2001.

Chappell, Bryan. *Each for the Other.* Grand Rapids: Baker, 2000.

Christenson, Evelyn. *What Happens When We Pray for Our Families*. Wheaton, Ill.: Chariot, 1992.

Lawson, Steven J. *The Legacy: What Every Father Wants to Leave His Child*. Sisters, Ore.: Multnomah, 1998.

Lewis, Frank. *Team Builder Book*. Nashville: Lifeway, 2000.

Luter, Boyd, and Kathy McReynolds. *Disciplined Living: What the New Testament Teaches About Recovery and Discipleship*. Grand Rapids: Baker, 1996.

MacArthur, John. *What the Bible Says About Parenting.* Dallas: Word, 2000.

Malphurs, Aubrey. *Developing a Vision for Ministry in the 21st Century.* Grand Rapids: Baker, 1992.

McIntosh, Gary. *Three Generations.* Grand Rapids: Baker, 1997.

Omartian, Stormie. *The Power of a Praying Parent.* Orlando: Harvest House, 1995.

Osborne, Rick, and John Trent. *Christian Parent's Guide to the Spiritual Growth of Children.* Carol Stream, Ill.: Tyndale, 2001.

Parrott, Les and Leslie. *Relationships.* Grand Rapids: Zondervan, 1998.

Silvoso, Ed. *That None Should Perish: How to Reach Entire Cities for Christ Through Prayer Evangelism.* Ventura, Calif.: Regal, 1994.

Notes

1. John P. Newport, "The Purpose of the Church," in *The People of God*, ed. Paul A. Basden and David S. Dockery (Nashville: Broadman & Holman, 1991), 27.
2. Millard J. Erickson, *Christian Theology* (Grand Rapids: Baker, 1998), 1063–64.
3. Wayne Grudem, *Systematic Theology* (Grand Rapids: Zondervan, 1994), 894.
4. C. Peter Wagner, *The Healthy Church* (Ventura, Calif.: Regal, 1996), 89–103.
5. Neil T. Anderson and Charles Mylander, *Setting Your Church Free* (Ventura, Calif.: Regal, 1994), 196.
6. See www.churchofmodesto.org.
7. The two previous statistics are from Barna Research Online, "Family."
8. The two previous statistics are from William Bennett, *The Broken Hearth* (Colorado Springs: Waterbrook, 2001), 12–13.
9. Ibid., 16–17.

CHAPTER 9

Leading in Change Without Losing the Battle

George Washington. Ulysses S. Grant. William T. Sherman. John J. Pershing. Dwight D. Eisenhower. George Patton. Norman Schwarzkopf. Colin Powell. . . . Leaders in Colonial Army and United States war efforts, from the Revolution in the 1700s to the Persian Gulf War in 1991.

We remember such men because they took charge and led their troops into battle and ultimately to victory. In times of military conflict, leaders are essential. If no one leads, or if the assumed leader has no plan, the troops are vulnerable to defeat—possibly at great loss of life.

Battles in the spiritual realm are no different, especially for churches that want to grow discipled warriors. If there is no leader, or if the assumed leader has no strategy, the church is seriously exposed to the arrows of the Enemy. On the other hand, an effective leader who wears the armor of God and equips members will lead the church to victory.

I assume that you want to be part of a healthy congregation that produces discipled warriors. This chapter will give basic directions for leaders who want to counter the typical roadblocks that the Enemy lays on the path to armed and ready congregational life.

Pray and Enlist Others to Pray

A survey conducted by church growth expert C. Peter Wagner discovered that the pastors surveyed pray an average of twenty-two minutes per day.[1] Twenty-eight percent of those surveyed said that they prayed under ten minutes per day. If these findings are anywhere close to reality, we can assume that the prayer life of most pastors isn't alarming the Enemy. Why do many leaders struggle with maintaining a consistent prayer life? Perhaps pastors allow themselves to become too busy. They spend so much time visiting, counseling, ministering, and preaching that prayer gets little attention. Some pastors and elders just don't have the discipline to pray consistently.

Maybe the real reason many leaders don't pray much is that we think we can handle ministry on our own. "Go ahead," the Enemy says to us, "Do ministry in your own strength. You're good enough. You know what to do and how to do it." The words of James Wilson, a pastor in Seaside, California, ring true:

> I've seen it at times in my own life: Need a moving sermon on prayer? I can preach it. Need me to pray for you? I can clear my throat, put my hand on your shoulder and comfort you with eloquent words. Look me in the eye and ask me, "How's your prayer life?" and I'll put my hands in my pockets, shift my weight, look away, and skillfully change the subject. A by-product of pride, prayerlessness grows when a pastor relies on himself rather than God.[2]

We don't like to admit it, but prayerlessness usually indicates that we don't really feel the need for God. We are not so blatant as Lucifer to say, "I will make myself like the Most High" (Isa. 14:14), but our underlying attitude speaks the same message.

Three steps help you to stand firm. *First, ask God to give you a prayer partner with whom you can be completely honest about your independent spirit.* Confess your lack of dependence on God, and let that truthfulness become a first step toward correcting the problem. The Enemy is dislodged when we bring our failures into the light.

Second, ask God to make you needy. None of us wants a thorn such as Paul experienced (2 Cor. 12:7), but that thorn kept Paul dependent on God. Surely his struggle kept him in prayer, and the apostle ultimately found strength in his weakness. If you want to become a prayer warrior whose ministry produces discipled warriors, ask God to make you weak rather than strong.

Third, ask your prayer partner to hold you accountable for praying. My accountability partners have permission to ask me at any time, "Have you prayed today?" Give your partners that permission and expect them to ask. While you do not want to pray *only because* you're held accountable, knowing that others will ask is a motivation. The obedience of prayer itself weakens the Enemy's influence.

Perhaps you remember how Moses led the Israelites in battle against the Amalekites (Exod. 17:8–16). Moses watched the battle from atop the hill, and the Israelites prevailed as long as he raised his staff. When he tired and lowered his staff, the Amalekites prevailed. Aaron and Hur came to Moses' side and supported his hands so that Joshua and his troops ultimately won the battle.

Leaders need that kind of support for their prayers. Ask God to give you someone who will help you hold your arms up in prayer. Ask Him to show you that you can't do ministry alone. Lead from your knees if you want to grow a church with discipled warriors.

Be Sure to Wear the Armor

The armor of God in Ephesians 6:11–18 is not some mystical set of incantations that we "pray on" every day. Paul's point was that simply faithful Christian living is effective in undermining the Enemy. We wear the armor when we walk in obedience. Church leaders who are not obedient aren't wearing the armor. In some cases, they're living in hidden disobedience, listening to the Enemy's voice saying, "Go ahead. Nobody'll know." Secret sin is destroying their lives.

In other cases, leaders are living in what I call "a state of unintended neglect," regarding spiritual disciplines. Bible study is inconsistent. Prayer is sporadic. Evangelism is nonexistent. These leaders are often still busy doing ministry, but their busyness has crowded out spiritual growth.

In either case—blatant sin or unintended neglect—the leader isn't armed to lead troops into the spiritual battle. Undisciplined leaders don't produce discipled warriors.

Use Exhibit 9-1 to analyze your own walk with the Lord. The evaluation questions are designed to help you make specific application with each piece of the armor.

Remember that Paul told us to wear the "full" armor of God (Eph. 6:11). If there are areas of your life where the armor is not apparent, take time to confess your vulnerable spots. Turn from any wrong so that the Enemy has no place to get a foothold. Become a leader whose obedience is a witness to others who face daily battles with the Enemy.

Follow Basic Principles for Leading

Change almost always produces conflict, as the following congregations will testify:

- The area surrounding church A had changed so drastically that the leaders thought that relocation was the best move for future growth. Younger members affirmed the move because they were uncomfortable reaching out to the changing minority around the neighborhood. Longer-

Exhibit 9-1 Putting on the Armor

Armor	Interpretation/Application	Evaluation
belt of truth	• Know Christ, who is Truth. • Trust the truth of Scripture. • Live truth with honesty and integrity.	Am I the same in private as when others watch? Do I live my faith and the Word?
breastplate of righteousness	• Be grateful for God's righteousness. • Live in holiness. • Imitate God in choices.	Do I stand firm when tempted? Does my daily life reflect righteousness?
feet shod with the gospel of peace	• Stand firm in faith. • Be ready to share faith. • Go where God calls. • Proclaim God's peace in midst of spiritual battles.	Do I use opportunities to tell others about Jesus and their need to be reconciled to Him?
shield of faith	• Know God's promises. • Trust Him to keep promises. • Act in keeping with faith.	Am I willing to obey, despite difficulty or opposition?
helmet of salvation	• Having accepted salvation, live in hope. • Know who you are in Christ. • Think differently than the world thinks.	Do I hope in Christ or give up easily? Is God honored by my thought life?
sword of the Spirit	• Know the Word of God. • Proclaim and teach it.	Do I study God's Word each day? Do I teach His Word or mine?

term members fought the change because they loved the building.

- Church B faced the unexpected resignation of a popular associate pastor. The associate left on good terms, but rumors flew, and several families left the church because they wrongly believed that the pastor had asked the associate to resign.

- Church C recently began meeting in their new worship center. They had prayed and sacrificed for this building for years. Now some members are complaining. The music is too loud. Screens make the place look like a movie theater. Churches should have pews, not padded seats. What happened to the hymnals?

In each of these cases, change created stress and anxiety—and ultimately, turmoil in the church. Look at Exhibit 9-2 to see how the Enemy often capitalizes on the stresses brought by change. Our reactions to change aren't always positive. Satan then lurks about, seeking to capitalize on those who react negatively. He waits to devour people who are struggling to adjust.

Exhibit 9-2 The Enemy and Change

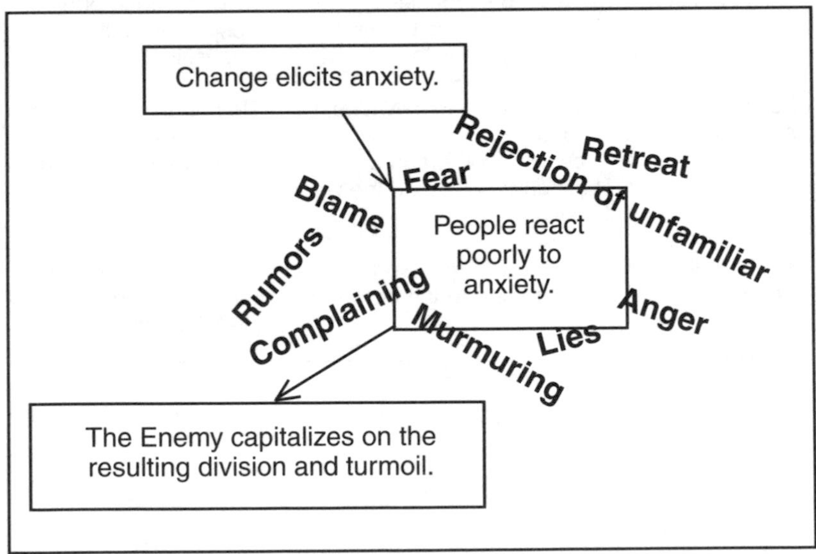

Many leaders want to lead through change, but they haven't thought through the intricate process for doing so successfully. If they lead poorly through change, the door is open for the Enemy to get a foothold. Leaders who attempt change without thinking take foolish and unnecessary risks, perhaps unintentionally following the Enemy's message to Jesus: "Go ahead. Jump from the temple. God will protect you."

Some leaders push for change without gaining the support of the followers. Others promote programs that worked elsewhere, without noticing differences in situation and context. Some have been known to claim divine authority for the change, almost daring members not to get on board. Others ride the waves of the latest fads, without a thought-out long-term vision.

Each of these leadership failures usually causes division. Some members feel threatened by rapid changes, while others feel ignored. The Enemy, of course, takes advantage of such opportunities.

One simple way to counter the Enemy's attacks is to follow basic principles for facilitating change. Take note of the following ideas if you want to lead your church through change safely.

Before attempting change, evaluate the risk carefully.[3] Ask these questions prior to making a move:

- *How much change do I have in my pocket?* Do I have the support necessary to lead through this change? Does the church trust my leadership enough to follow me? If the change is ineffective, do I have enough credibility to remain the leader in spite of the failure?
- *What's the worst thing that can happen if the change doesn't work?* Can I live with it? Is the change so important that I'm willing to take significant risks to accomplish it?
- *Who else has done it?* What can we learn from those who have made this change? How can we avoid their mistakes?
- *Who wields the influence and must be "on board"?* Every church

has a shadow government of significant leaders whose support is required if change is to succeed.

- *What is my strategy for selling the change?* Do I have a plan to help the people catch the vision? How will I lead them *to* and then *through* it?
- *How clearly has God spoken?* Leaders who aren't convinced of God's direction won't stay focused during opposition. How certain am I that God is behind this change?

Be willing to eat the elephant one bite at a time. One of the best books I know on leading an established church through change is *Eating the Elephant.*[4] Author Thom Rainer argues that the best way to lead a church through change is the same way to eat an elephant: *one bite at a time.* Tackling too much at one time leads only to frustration and defeat.

Gene Appel, pastor of Central Christian Church in Henderson, Nevada, in over fifteen years as pastor, has led his church in growth from 450 to more than 5000 attendees. Changes have been numerous, including adding services and introducing contemporary music into the services. Over the years, Pastor Appel has learned that "beginning incrementally and respecting the readiness of the congregation were two keys that unlocked the door to major and lasting change."[5] Slow change has been positive change.

Our research at the Billy Graham School indicates that pastors of evangelistically growing churches have an average tenure that is more than three times the national average (11.8 years versus 3.8 years).[6] It seems likely to me that these pastors recognize the importance of "eating the elephant" one bite at a time. They know that change takes time, and they commit the time necessary for the change to be promoted, understood, and adopted.

Lead your church to change as necessary, *but do it well.* Don't expect God to catch you if you foolishly leap into more trouble simply because you have not followed good principles for change.

Get Some Troops on Board

Few people want to face a battle alone. When the war rages around us, we like to know that there are others fighting alongside us. Sometimes it seems as though nobody else is willing to enter the battle. Maybe you know what changes are needed in your church, but nobody supports you. You've tried to raise the standards, but other leaders buck the proposed changes. In the end, you want to give up and cry out with Elijah hiding in the cave, "I alone am left" (1 Kings 19:10).

How do you lead to victory when it seems easier to retreat to the cave?

First, hear God's *response* to Elijah.

Elijah was fleeing Queen Jezebel when God found him in the cave. The battle the prophet faced was real, and Elijah despaired. Satan knows that isolated warriors don't stay in the battle very long. God quickly showed Elijah that he was one of *seven thousand* (1 Kings 19:18). God's army was bigger than Elijah thought. The prophet just needed to learn that truth–and so do we when we think that we fight the battles alone.

On a rainy September day in 1814, British ships shelled Fort McHenry in the Baltimore harbor. The bombardment continued through the night, with little return fire from the fort's guns. The fort seemed ready to fall. The next morning, Francis Scott Key, a lawyer on a ship eight miles from the fort, peered through his telescope. Above Fort McHenry he saw an American flag flying. A wet flag had been replaced during the night, and the fresh flag indicated that Fort McHenry had not fallen. The troops were still fighting. That simple sign of a flag inspired Key to set down "The Star-Spangled Banner."

As you lead toward growth, know that there will be times when it appears that the fort is about to fall. When those times come, ask God to remind you that you're not alone. Raise high the Christian flag, and press on.

Second, remember that change *takes* place one life at a time. If your goal is to get the whole church on board with a new direction, you'll probably fail. Even Jesus did not get everybody on board. What Jesus did do was change one life at a time. He called Zaccheus from the tree (Luke 19:1–10), Matthew from the tax collector's booth (Matt. 9:9), Simon and Andrew from their nets (Mark 1:16–18), and a woman from the well (John 4:1–29). He changed His world by changing individual lives.

That's the way God typically uses us to change congregations—*one life at a time.* Equip a few warriors, and challenge them to equip a few others. Work individually with current leaders to gain their support. Make the investment necessary to get the influential leaders on board. Take the Enemy's land little by little, one by one.

This overall process takes some time, but a few well-trained troops are better than many who haven't really been prepared for the battle. The discipled warriors might be outnumbered at first, but they will be ready to march forward.

Third, with the support of the prayer warriors, rally the troops around God's mission. Luke 9:28–36 tells of Jesus' "transfiguration." There, before three of His disciples, Jesus was changed. His face shone, and His clothing became white and glistening. Moses and Elijah even appeared and spoke with Him. Affirmed by the Father's voice, Jesus stood robed in glory—yet the topic of His conversation with Moses and Elijah was His coming death. He would reign in glory, but not without enduring the cross. His mission was clear, and nothing would deter Him.

That's the resolve He expects from His body as we make disciples of all the world. Get the prayer warriors praying for persistence, and challenge the people to march on to fulfill the Great Commission. God can change a congregation with a few people committed to overcoming the Enemy.

Pray for Discontent with the Status Quo

The problem with most churches that need to change is *not* that they don't want to be warriors. They just don't see a need for change. They get comfortable where they are and settle into routines no one should disturb. Complacent, they fail to see themselves as they really are.

The church at Laodicea was like that (Rev. 3:14–22). They saw themselves as rich, but they were really "wretched, pitiful, poor, blind and naked" (v. 17 NIV). Jesus' words imply that they were blind to the truth that they were complacent, satisfied, and unconcerned about matters of faith (v. 18).

Strong words from Jesus were needed to shock them out of their apathy: "So because you are lukewarm, and neither hot nor cold, I will spit you out of My mouth" (v. 16). Only when the Laodiceans recognized their need would they repent. They needed to know Jesus' distaste for their condition.

We tend not to accept change until we see the need. A wise leader guides toward discomfort. Indeed, good leaders never allow people to be entirely happy with where they are. The Enemy wants to see them comfortable with the status quo, satisfied with nongrowth. Good leaders challenge the status quo when the church isn't growing. One such leader is Claude Payne, an Episcopal bishop in Texas, whose model for "reclaiming the Great Commission" has increased attendance, baptisms, lay participation, outreach, and giving in the Episcopal diocese of Texas.[7]

Bishop Payne first created a sense of urgency about the state of the Episcopal diocese and the needs of the surrounding community. He "relentlessly reminded the diocese about its problems, potential problems, and potential opportunities," especially regarding drops in attendance, church and denominational division, aging membership, and perceived irrelevance to a secular world.[8] In the end, urgency led the churches to realize that the status quo was unacceptable.

If you want your church to move toward health, join your prayer warriors and troops already on board to pray, "Lord, make our church uncomfortable with where we are." Consider some of the following ways to draw your church out of the comfort zone:

- Do a statistical analysis of the church's growth, especially patterns of plateau or decline. Show the findings graphically, especially when the church is in decline.
- Do a demographic study of the community to show the church the numbers of people who remain unreached. Increase the church's commitment to outreach by introducing them to the unchurched world.
- Acquaint the people with congregations that are reaching the unchurched. Read books about successes, and take laypersons to conferences sponsored by them. Challenge your church not to emulate others but to learn from them.
- Study biblical and historical accounts of revivals and awakenings. Under God's leadership, create a prayerful desire in your church for God to move in a powerful way.
- Enlist a prayer team to pray daily that the church never becomes comfortable.

As your prayer team prays against the church's comfort, encourage them to pray for unity in the church as well. A church that is never entirely comfortable is probably always experiencing a little chaos. Controlled chaos always risks opening the door to the Enemy, but discipled warriors close that door through prayer.

Ask God for His Plan

As was noted in chapter 2, we best overcome the Enemy's schemes not by reacting to him but by preparing for him. By making disciples, we arm believers to stand against the Enemy and resist him. Disciplemaking does not happen without planning. The sound church establishes and carries out an intentional discipleship plan that prepares them to stand when the Enemy attacks.

Regrettably, few churches have a strategic plan in place. There are reasons for this omission, none of which justify it:

- Some leaders don't know how to prepare a strategy. Seminary training often doesn't equip students in this significant area of leadership.
- Some leaders believe that planning gives the body a secular business orientation.
- The daily grind of ministry gets in the way of strategic planning. There aren't enough hours to complete today's work, much less think about tomorrow.
- Some pastors aren't willing to make a long-term commitment, because they are always thinking about jumping up to the *next* church.
- Other professionals are in "maintenance mode." They don't want to upset the calm and perhaps put their jobs in jeopardy by strategizing for future growth.

Whatever the reason for not strategizing, the danger is that the church faces an enemy who *does* have a plan. He devours bodies whose troops have no battle plan in place (1 Peter 5:8).

Let me clarify here that I don't believe most leaders intentionally choose not to have a strategic plan. I certainly don't think that leaders want their people to be vulnerable to the Enemy's attacks. But when a church does not have a strategic plan to fulfill its commission, for whatever reason, it is vulnerable. Intentionally or not, we listen to the Enemy's message, "Go ahead and build your church–just don't worry about finding God's way to get it done."

God has a plan for the world and for His people. He intentionally called out a kingdom of priests (Gen. 12:1–3; Exod.

19:5–6). He led the Israelites through the wilderness to build them according to His plan (Exod. 13:17). So they might worship Him, God also gave them detailed blueprints for a tabernacle (Exodus 25–30). Through the centuries, He guided and protected His people, from whom would come the Messiah. Indeed, God's plan was most evident as He sent His Son "when the fullness of the time came" (Gal. 4:4). Christ's coming was a carefully planned part of God's strategy.

Christ also gave a commission to the early church (Matt. 28:18–20). He designed a plan for reaching the world (Acts 1:8). Even now we follow a plan, trusting when we do not know all the details (Matt. 24:36; Acts 1:7). Doesn't it make sense that this strategically thinking God also has a plan for your church? What might happen if each part of Christ's body truly prayed, sought His plan, and implemented it well? The God who gave Joseph a plan to save His people from starvation (Genesis 41) still works from a strategy.

How do you determine God's strategy? Lead your church to pray and read God's Word. While this first step might seem simplistic, most churches *assume* prayer and Bible study more than they teach them. Lead your people to pray consistently as individuals and as the corporate body. Study God's Word together to understand God's desires.

Then, determine to be intentional and specific in planning. General planning seldom leads to action. Compare the plans in Exhibit 9-3 to recognize the value of specificity in strategic planning.

The Enemy is not alarmed by generic plans that never lead to specific accomplishments. He wants us to *think* that we are accomplishing something but never to enter the battle. How many churches have long-range plans that are gathering dust? Decide as church leaders that your planning will include specific goals, intentional direction, and clear action steps. Consider using the model in this book as a grid to guide your strategizing. Review the model of a healthy church (Exhibit 1-2, p. 25) and remember

Exhibit 9-3 General vs. Specific Planning

General plan	Specific plan
To reach the world for Christ.	We will send one short-term international mission team each year.
To evangelize lost people.	We will share the gospel in each subdivision of our community by visits, mailings, and block parties.
To increase financial stewardship.	We will increase giving 10 percent through intentional stewardship training in new member classes.
To influence our community.	We will develop a needs-based ministry outreach to migrant workers.

that Satan battles against all of these components. He uses false teachers to weaken theological foundations, and he strikes against efforts to fulfill each purpose. At the same time, the Enemy attacks us in our personal lives, in our homes, and in our workplaces.

To prepare for and ward off attacks, an overall strategy should address each component. While we "eat the elephant" one bite at a time, a good strategy helps us to know where to take the first spoonful. For example, a vigorous prayer focus is vital to ministry. Leaders should ask several questions about their prayer program. What are we doing to teach people what the Bible says about prayer? How are we preparing people to pray? What are we doing to guide members to pray for family or coworkers? Are they praying for the needs of the world?

To meet deficiencies in prayer ministry, planning must be intentional and strategic. Exhibit 9-4 offers some sample planning forms regarding the purpose of evangelism to show this process in action.

Exhibit 9-4 Sample Planning Sheets

Goals

Purpose of the church: EVANGELISM

Primary goals for the year:

1. To teach a biblical view of evangelism.
2. To involve 50 percent of members in some form of evangelism.
3. To train 25 percent of young parents to share Christ with their own children.
4. To prepare members for workplace witness.

Action Plan

Purpose of the church: EVANGELISM

Specific goal: To train 25 percent of young parents to share Christ with their own children.

Action Plan # ____: One-day child evangelism seminar for parents.

Date: Saturday, April 25

Time: 9:00 A.M. to 12:00 P.M.

Person responsible: Children's ministry director

Facilities required: Fellowship Hall

Resources/equipment required: Power-point data projector.

Budget: $200 for materials and publicity.

Publicity Plan: Flyers, packets for attendees.

Follow up: Phone calls/visits if indicated by children's ministry director. Contact information to outreach coordinator.

Measurable objectives: Attendees will go away with specific ideas and expressed excitement for discipling children. Church will give contact information and packet on church and its programs to parents from outside the congregation who do not attend elsewhere.

Healthy churches may use the model in this book to evaluate their ministry efforts, from building a solid theological foundation to living out their faith in the workplace. Dreaming, planning, implementing, evaluating, and improving should become part of the organizational DNA.

Even as I write this section, however, I can hear the complaints: "That's a lot of work, isn't it?" "I don't have time to do all that planning." "We don't have enough laypersons to do all that." "Our church doesn't think that far ahead." "Why can't we just keep doing what we're doing?" "Do you mean we have to do this kind of planning for everything we do?"

Strategizing and planning are hard work, but a God-directed strategy gives tools to win the battles of spiritual warfare. Discover God's strategy and follow it. Not to strategize and plan is to give the Devil an open door.

Lead as a Servant

Brother Jack Tichenor was a pastor of congregations in Kentucky, Tennessee, and Ohio for almost sixty years. "Brother Jack" led growing churches throughout his ministry. He served in significant denominational positions. He was well known, deeply loved, and respected. But what I remember most about Brother Jack was his servant spirit. He often spoke about having a "sweetheart love for Jesus," and he modeled that love for Christ and others. Many of us went to him for advice, but never did I hear him say a negative word about anyone. Nor was there an ounce of arrogance in him. Today, our seminary offers a scholarship that honors Jack's life. Students receive the continued blessings of his life, although I wish that the recipients of these funds could have known him. The Devil would be alarmed if more ministers had the servant heart of Jack Tichenor.

Jesus overcame the Enemy through servant leadership. He reached out to forgive a rejected woman, helping her break destructive relationships in her life (John 4:7–29). He had dinner with a hated tax collector, but then expected him to give back to those he had cheated (Luke 19:1–10). Jesus touched lepers whom no one else would touch (Matt. 8:2–4) and ministered to demoniacs whom everyone else feared (Mark 5:1–20). He paid the ultimate price of servanthood—obedience to death—so that lost people might be freed from the Enemy's grasp.

As a servant, He could with integrity demand that His followers become servants (Matt. 20:24–28). "If anyone wants to be first," Jesus said, "he shall be last of all and servant of all" (Mark 9:35). How contrary those words are to Lucifer's words when he sought to make himself "like the Most High" (Isa. 14:14).

Servant leaders are committed to Jesus, live like Jesus lived, and lead like Jesus led. Calvin Miller describes such commitment this way:

> Great spiritual leaders do not stop us with their reputation, but with their devotion to His inescapable importance. . . . They are unable to live without the Savior. He absorbs all their interest, dictates their need, and beckons them to His agenda. . . . Servant leaders generally are created not in commanding others but in obeying their Commander. In such a mystique, executive arrogance is not possible. The yielded leader is always an incarnation of Christ, the real leader of His church.[9]

This kind of leader follows God without regard to self, and that spirit frustrates an enemy who is himself self-centered and arrogant. The Devil and humble servanthood seldom stay in the same room for very long.

Application

Abraham Lincoln led the United States during a critical time. Not everyone agreed with Lincoln's leadership style or decisions, but few people questioned his commitment to doing whatever was necessary to preserve the United States. In the end, he gave his life. If Lincoln so stood for an earthly cause, how much more should Christian leaders stand for God's cause? Be the leader that God has called you to be–*stand for Him* as you grow discipled warriors in your church. Perhaps the following ideas will help you to strengthen your leadership in the battle:

- Study great leaders of the Bible. Begin with a study of Jesus' methods of leadership. Preach on biblical leadership.
- Develop leader mentors.
- Evaluate current ministry with the diaconate, session, or board in relation to the model presented in this book. Determine what needs improving, and plan to make those improvements.
- Enlist prayer warriors to uphold leaders, including yourself. If you are a pastor, meet with them monthly to update them on pastoral and elder-deacon needs.
- Once a quarter, read a biography or autobiography of a significant leader. Consider beginning a book club with others.
- Budget for and plan to attend an annual leadership conference at a growing church. Talk to those who have grown churches successfully, learning from their successes and failures.
- Survey to seek indications of the comfort level with the "status quo." One resource is the *Church Health Survey* available through ChurchCentral, Inc.[10]
- Prepare leaders to understand the process of change before launching a change initiative.
- Survey leaders to determine whether they need more training to be effective.
- Enlist a "strategic planning" committee. Work with ministry leaders to coordinate the church's overall ministry efforts.

- One ministry at a time, work through the planning sheets suggested in this chapter.

For further study

Barna, George, ed. *Leaders on Leadership*. Ventura, Calif.: Regal, 1997.

Blackaby, Henry, and Richard Blackaby. *Spiritual Leadership*. Nashville: Broadman & Holman, 2001.

Carter, Les, and Jim Underwood. *The Significance Principle*. Nashville: Broadman & Holman, 1998.

Clinton, Robert. *The Making of a Leader.* Colorado Springs, Col.: NavPress, 1988.

Collins, Jim. *Good to Great.* New York: HarperBusiness, 2001.

Guinness, Os. *The Call*. Nashville: Word, 1998.

MacArthur, John. *Rediscovering Pastoral Ministry*. Dallas: Word, 1995.

Maxwell, John C. *Developing the Leader Within You.* Nashville: Thomas Nelson, 1993.

Miller, Herb, ed. *Leadership Is the Key*. Nashville: Abingdon, 1997.

Phillips, Donald T. *The Founding Fathers on Leadership*. New York: Warner, 1997.

Sanders, J. Oswald. *Spiritual Leadership*. Chicago: Moody, 1980.

Shelley, Marshall, ed. *Growing Your Church Through Evangelism and Outreach.* Nashville: Moorings, 1996.

Spurgeon, Charles. *Lectures to My Students*. Grand Rapids: Zondervan, 1954.

Stowell, Joseph. *Shepherding the Church.* Chicago: Moody, 1997.

Wofford, Jerry C. *Transforming Christian Leadership*. Grand Rapids: Baker, 1999.

Notes

1. C. Peter Wagner, *PrayerShield* (Ventura: Regal, 1992), 78–79.
2. Jim Wilson, "Nominations from the Floor: More Candidates for Ministry's Eighth Deadly Sin," *Leadership* 22.2 (Spring 2001): 46.

3. Most of these questions are taken from Larry Osborne, "Before You Risk," in *Empowering Your Church Through Creativity and Change* (Nashville: Moorings, 1995), 149–58.
4. Thom Rainer, *Eating the Elephant* (Nashville: Broadman & Holman, 1993).
5. Alan Nelson and Gene Appel, *How to Change Your Church* (Nashville: Word, 2000), 73.
6. Thom S. Rainer, *Surprising Insights from the Unchurched* (Grand Rapids: Zondervan, 2001), 146.
7. Claude E. Payne and Hamilton Beazley, *Reclaiming the Great Commission* (San Francisco: Jossey-Bass, 2000).
8. Ibid., 95.
9. Calvin Miller, *The Empowered Leader* (Nashville: Broadman & Holman, 1995), 17–18.
10. Go to www.churchcentral.com.

CHAPTER 10

A Concluding Challenge

Not all stories of spiritual warfare in the Bible are stories of effective or victorious warriors. To the contrary, sometimes we learn what these heroes did wrong. Some were incredibly *ineffective*. It might seem strange to end this book by examining some negatives, but they challenge our thinking. Those who want to produce discipled warriors should learn from these failures.

Don't Fight Today's Battles in Yesterday's Strength

The first story is the Transfiguration of Jesus in Mark 9:1–9. Jesus had taken Peter, James, and John to the top of a mountain, where He prayed. There He was supernaturally changed, and He stood before them in His glory. And that wasn't all—Moses and Elijah joined Him.

Peter was so awed that he could not think clearly, but he thought that he should be saying or doing *something* at this unique visitation. "Let's build tabernacles," he said to the Lord. "One for Elijah, one for Moses, and one for You." It was the sort of commemoration that religious people raised to mark such mighty acts of God (e.g., Gen. 12:7; 28:10–22). Impulsive, excitable, and yet devoted to the Lord, Peter just wanted to respond appropriately to make this event permanent. It was not every day that the disciples got a glimpse of Jesus' divine glory, nor was it commonplace for Moses and Elijah to drop by.

Jesus, though, wouldn't let the men raise memorials or stay on the mountain. He understood that God's plan still required His death in Jerusalem (Luke 9:31). At that moment, too, a spiritual warfare problem was discouraging His followers at the foot of the mountain. In the valley, a desperate father had asked the disciples to heal his son's seizures. They had tried and failed to cast a demon from the boy. Challenged by the Enemy's power, they lost the spiritual warfare battle. Jesus was that father's last hope.

Jesus, as the "last hope," is still the best hope, however. He returned from the mountain, confronted the demonic spirit, exorcised it, and freed the boy. What His disciples could not do, Jesus did easily.

Some time later His disciples asked why they had failed against this demonic authority. "This kind," Jesus answered, "can come out only by prayer" (Mark 9:29 NIV). The disciples had not done what they needed to do—*pray*. Apparently, they had taken on the Enemy in their own strength. The result was obvious failure, with a little boy still possessed and his father even more discouraged.

We can't know for certain why the disciples didn't pray as they should have, but here's one possible reason. They had previously been successful at casting out demons (Mark 6:7–13), and maybe they thought that yesterday's power was still enough to fight today's battles. If we assume that yesterday's victories assure us of victory today, then why pray again? The disciples learned the hard way, though, that they couldn't fight spiritual battles today on the basis of yesterday's victories.

That lesson is important if you would lead an armed church that wins spiritual battles. Yesterday's victories are important in the history of your church, but they don't guarantee victory today. The Enemy fires new arrows every day, so daily we must put on the armor of God afresh. Satan will find an opening to invade our lives and churches if we let down our guard.

Never rejoice in warfare victories with the assumption that

you have now finally conquered and needn't pray as you once did. A fit church will quickly become unfit without prayer. Pray without ceasing (1 Thess. 5:17), and produce discipled warriors who do the same.

Recognize as well that the mountaintop experiences are great, but we can't stay up there when needy people wait at the foot of the mountain. God replenishes us on the heights so that we can better face the battles in the valley. Discipled warriors put their armor on and head into the battle.

At the same time, leading a church toward overcoming health can be exhausting work. The battles will be intense if your congregation takes the gospel into the darkness. As a discipled warrior seeking to produce other discipled warriors, know when you need renewal on the mountain. Sometimes we need to retreat from the valley and head back up the mountain to be renewed and refreshed. We especially need to head there when our prayer life needs strengthening. Our goal should be balance between the mountaintop and the valley, between renewal and the place where the needy people live.

Don't Take on the Enemy Unarmed

The second story of failed spiritual warfare is found in Acts 19:11–17. Paul had been teaching in Ephesus, a city whose paganism was dominated by worship of the goddess Diana (Artemis). Attention to spiritual powers was prominent.

Seven exorcists, sons of a Jewish rabbi named Sceva, were in the city. When they came upon a demon-possessed man, they tried to cast out the demon in the name of Jesus whom Paul preached (Acts 19:13). The evil spirit not only didn't obey the command; he asked sarcastically, "Jesus I know, and Paul I know; but who are ye?" (19:15 KJV). In a fit of defiance, the spirit led the possessed man to beat the sons of Sceva.

Think about the question: "Jesus I know, and Paul I know, but who are you?" The evil spirit knew Jesus because He was the Son of God. He knew Paul because Paul walked with God. Why did he not know the sons of Sceva? They had the words but not the divine authority, and nothing in their lives had raised panic in the demonic realm. They lacked authority and the protective armor of God.

The result was a frightening failure.

Many spiritual warfare enthusiasts today are fascinated with identifying and naming demons to overcome them. Indeed, people spend thousands of dollars on prayer journeys to identify a stronghold over a given region. That strategy, in my opinion, is misdirected.

Spiritual warfare isn't about naming demons; it's about so living a righteous life that our very life threatens the Enemy. We needn't know the names of demons; what matters is that the demons know us because Christ lives in us. Christian obedience shakes hell more than any attempts to name the demons.

At the same time, conducting spiritual warfare by formula simply doesn't work. The sons of Sceva had heard that Jesus and Paul had power over the Enemy, and they tried to use those names in a formulaic way. They recited the words but lacked the power.

Some people approach spiritual warfare with a formula, claiming the name of Jesus over the demons, assuming that just reciting the name *Jesus* will ensure victory. That didn't work so well for the sons of Sceva. Others use model prayers to overcome demons for every sin they face. Still other people have established routines for confronting and removing demonic influences. Spiritual warfare is not about learning a formula to overcome the Enemy; it is instead about *living a life* that gives the Enemy no place to get a foothold. Obedience, rather than ritual, overcomes the Enemy.

Here's my concern: Many people are enamored of the power and excitement of spiritual warfare, but leaders aren't often calling them first to holiness and obedient living. They are trying to be warriors without first being discipled. Acts 19 shows us clearly that that position is dangerous. To take on the Enemy without wearing the armor of God is foolish indeed.

Healthy churches, on the other hand, strive to grow discipled warriors. They build a theological foundation, fulfill the purposes of the church, and guide members to flesh out their faith in their personal walk, in their homes, in the church, and in their workplaces. In the end, they lead a congregation whose names the Enemy recognizes—and fears.

Grow this kind of church. Produce discipled warriors who defeat the Enemy.

Subject Index

Scripture Index